Needlepoint
1/12 Scale
DESIGN COLLECTIONS FOR THE DOLLS' HOUSE

Needlepoint
1/12 Scale
DESIGN COLLECTIONS FOR THE DOLLS' HOUSE

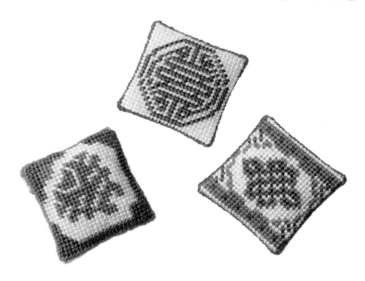

Felicity Price

Guild of Master Craftsman Publications Ltd

*This book is dedicated, with love, to the memory of
my mother, Irene Norman, who was unfailing in her
encouragement and shared my fascination with all things
small. The little blue cot blanket in the nursery was knitted
by her for my own dolls' house.*

First published 2000
by Guild of Master Craftsman Publications Ltd
Castle Place, 166 High Street, Lewes
East Sussex BN7 1XU

Copyright © GMC Publications Ltd

Text and charts copyright © Felicity Price

Reprinted 2001

Photography by Anthony Bailey

Cover photography by Andrew Southon

Dolls' house shown on page 3 kindly supplied by Laurenz Puddick, made
from a Toy Workshop kit

A catalogue record of this book is available from the British Library.

ISBN 1 86108 166 9

Designed and edited by Christopher and Gail Lawther

Colour origination by Viscan Graphics Pte Ltd (Singapore)
Printed in China by Sun Fung Offset Binding Co Ltd

CONTENTS

These glimpses inside our dolls' house show each room's unique design collection, plus a selection of the tools and materials used to produce them.

INTRODUCTION

The world of miniatures has expanded tremendously in the past few years. Thirty years ago, if you had told people that you collected miniatures they would have assumed that you meant small paintings, or even small bottles of exotic liqueurs. Now, of course, the word miniatures is most frequently associated with dolls' houses; the idea covers not only the collecting of tiny treasures, old and new, but also the vast arena of creative skills which you can use to create your own miniatures.

The pleasure of creativity

I'm convinced that each of us has the ability to create something for our own dolls' house. Some people are a whizz with that fiddly Fimo food, and others can produce a masterpiece of furniture with just a few tools, but for me there's nothing quite like the pleasure of sitting in a sunny corner and doing a little needlepoint.

From start to finish…

Even if you've never done any needlepoint before, you'll find everything you need to know in the Basic Guide to Stitching (beginning on page 10), and the Basic Guide to Finishing (beginning on page 16); these give detailed instructions on how to stitch the projects and complete your work. The project chapters cover a wide range of items aimed at different levels of stitching expertise; in my choice of projects I've tried to show the many different ways in which you can use needlepoint throughout your dolls' house, and I hope they offer something for everyone.

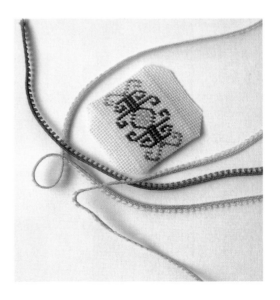

The stitched items themselves range from easy through to demanding, and from frivolous to formal; overall they offer small and large projects in a rainbow of colours. The easiest projects are grouped near the beginning of the book, and the ones towards the end are more challenging. The designs in each project chapter are presented as a complementary collection, so that you can develop a theme in your miniature room, and at the end of each chapter you'll also find further suggestions for colour or project variations, so that you can create a piece of stitching to harmonize with your own colour-schemes or the particular style of your own dolls' house.

Background information

Alongside the patterns and instructions in each section I've also provided some background to the design and the historical use of each type of room. Of course for the scope of a book like this the historical detail is inevitably condensed and generalized, but I've tried to present an accurate overall picture so that you can fix your miniature room into a particular era. The introductory sections also give you something to think about while you're stitching, and may spur you on to further research.

Personalizing your second home

For centuries needlepoint has been used in the home to create carpets, wall-hangings, bed-hangings, cushions, chair coverings and much more, so it seems very appropriate that we use it in our dolls' houses – those unique little homes that we create so carefully. The needlepoint projects in this book are intended to help you create personal and individual treasures for your house. Needlework treasures on which nobody will wipe their muddy feet or spill their coffee – surely one of the main pleasures of our 'second' homes!

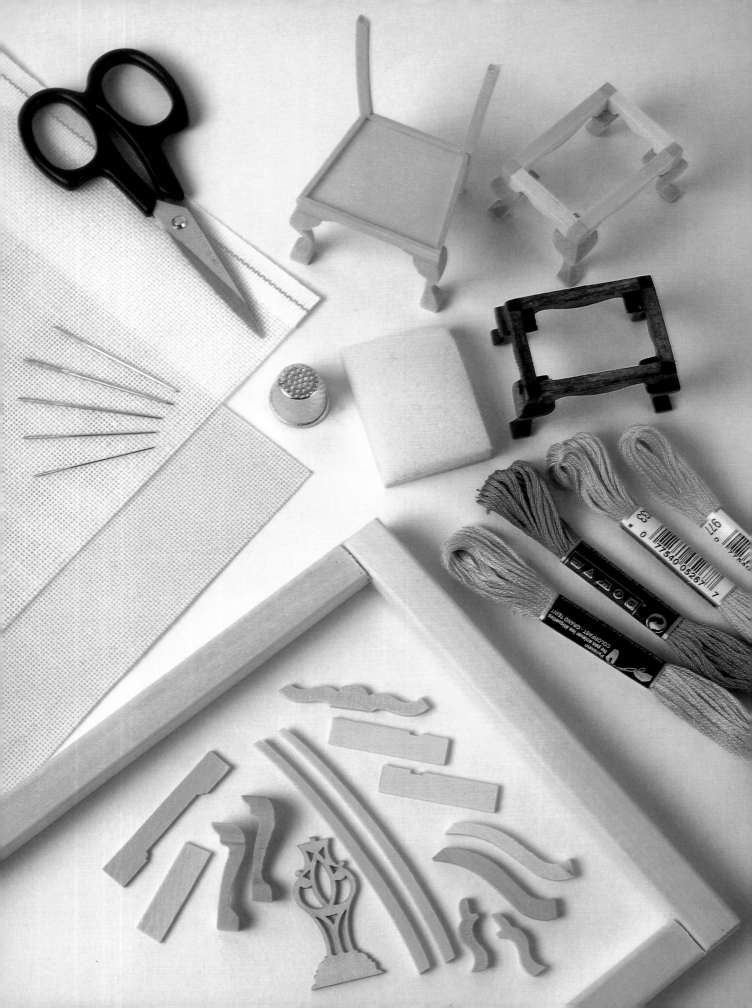

BASIC GUIDES

*T*his is the essential 'How to…' section necessary in every craft book. I must confess that I often neglect this part of a book until some horrible difficulty has arisen and I'm pretty close to throwing a tantrum worthy of any two-year-old – and I don't imagine for one moment that I'm alone in this. After all, how many of us sit and read the manuals that come with a new washing machine, car or computer?

If you have previous experience of 1/12th scale needlepoint patterns then most of this information will already be familiar to you, but sometimes it's worth reinforcing the detail with a quick read-through.

If you've already stitched real-size 'tapestry' cushions or pictures for your own home, then you will know the mechanics of stitching but probably won't have stitched anything so small. In this case you'd be wise to read through the Basic Guide to Materials section (see page 6), as all the materials have to be scaled down for 1/12th scale miniatures, and also the Basic Guide to Finishing section (see page 16), as techniques for working with tiny things are sometimes different.

If you're accustomed to stitching small items but have previously only worked them in cross stitch, then please do read the Basic Guide to Stitching (see page 10), as the patterns in this book are designed for basketweave, petitpoint or half-cross stitch and will not be the same if worked in cross stitch.

If you have never stitched before in your life – don't be afraid! This section will help you with each stage – from selecting your materials, through making your first stitch, and all the way to finishing your project.

Basic Guide to Materials

There are only two materials used for all these designs – the canvas, and the thread. However, before selecting these we need to give a little thought to scale.

Scale

The designs in this book are intended for 1/12th scale, which is the most popular size for collectors' dolls' houses and miniatures. This is also known as the 'inch to a foot' scale; it's really very easy to work with, and you don't have to be a mathematician or use a calculator to work out your sizes. Each foot of a life-size object simply becomes an inch in the new scale. So, if you have a rug on the floor in your own home which is 4ft long by 3ft wide, then the equivalent size in a dolls' house would be 4 inches long by 3 inches wide.

Canvas

The canvas is the woven material on which you're going to make your stitches. Although this can be made from linen, cotton or silk, for these projects I recommend using cotton canvas in a white, cream or ecru (off white) colour. If you don't use a frame (see Basic Guide to Tools, page 8), then the canvas is going to be handled a great deal while you're working on it and the edges may fray quite badly; therefore I recommend a strong cotton canvas, which will minimize fraying and also hold its shape while you're stitching. If you prefer to use a softer canvas then you might try binding the edges with adhesive masking tape to prevent them from fraying.

Canvas thread counts

Now you need to concentrate. The thread count of the canvas is very important. The designs in this book are intended for 22 tpi count canvas. This means that if you measure one inch of canvas you will be able to count 22 threads (or 22 holes). If you use canvas with a different tpi then your finished project will come out a different size.

So using 22 tpi canvas, if you stitch up a rug which is 88 stitches long and 66 stitches wide, then you know that the finished rug size will be 4 inches by 3 inches. (You calculate this by dividing the number of stitches by the thread count of the canvas: eg, 88 sts divided by 22 tpi = 4 inches.)

Now, suppose you find a piece of 18 tpi canvas in your sewing box and decide to use it up, stitching the same design of 88 x 66 stitches. Then you can work out:

88 sts divided by 18 tpi = 4.8in, and

66 sts divided by 18 tpi = 3.6in

so your rug would end up as 4.8 x 3.6 inches, slightly larger than the original project measurements.

From these calculations you can see that the smaller the tpi or thread count of your canvas, the larger your finished work will be. This may all sound very complicated, but if you stick to 22 tpi canvas throughout the book then the finished sizes will be as given for each project, and you don't need to clutter up your brain with working out variations!

COMMON
ABBREVIATIONS
tpi = threads per inch
hpi = holes per inch
sts = stitches

Stitching threads

The threads used for stitching the projects are far more exciting than the canvas, mainly because they come in such a beautiful array of colours. Miniature needlepoint can be stitched using cotton, wool or silk threads. Wool gives a slightly fluffy finish to your project and, to my mind, a 'matt' effect to the colours. Silk is rather more expensive and a little more difficult to work with, although the results are good.

Stranded cotton is very easy to work with, is available in a staggering choice of colours (over 450), provides a neat flat finish and gives a slightly silky sheen to your work. (In fact stranded cottons are often referred to as embroidery 'silks.') All the projects in this book are designed to be stitched using stranded cotton thread. The key for each project gives the colours from the Anchor range and their closest approximations in the DMC and Madeira ranges; there are slight variations between dyes – your needlework shop should be able to show you all the options from the different ranges.

Basic Guide to Tools

Unlike hobbies such as woodwork, pottery and mountaineering, miniature needlework needs no gadgets. The few tools it does require are both inexpensive and easy to carry around – which makes it, of course, the ideal hobby.

Essential tools

Only two things are essential: needles and scissors. You could get away with one needle but you must have a pair of scissors…

Needles for needlepoint are different from the ordinary sewing needles which you may already have in your workbox. Ordinary needles have to make their own holes in the fabric, so have to be sharp: in needlepoint, though, the needle passes through ready-made holes in the canvas, so a special rounded-tip tapestry needle is used. The blunt tip helps to prevent the needle from catching in your stitches – and also minimizes sore fingers. As with the canvas, tapestry needles come in a variety of sizes: for 22 tpi canvas I suggest you use a size 26 needle. To test whether your needle is the right size: make sure that you can thread three strands of stranded cotton easily through its eye, and that it will pass through a hole in your canvas without any effort on your part.

A small pair of *scissors* with sharp points is ideal (these are often called embroidery scissors). The points need to stay sharp so that they'll cut efficiently, so keep the scissors hidden from the rest of the family and, when asked if you have any – lie.

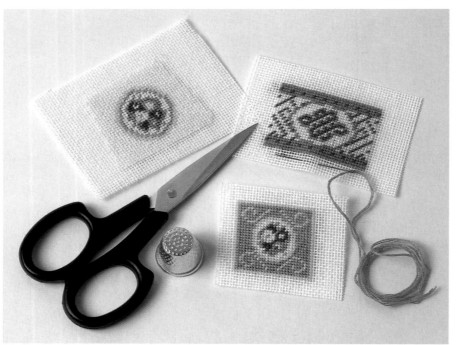

Tools that are non-essential but nice to have

Usually a needlepoint book will list a good *frame* under essentials. This is to keep the canvas taut while you are working and to prevent the stitched piece from pulling out of shape.

Various types of frame are available to suit different methods of working. A small lap frame is helpful, leaves both hands free and prevents distortion of larger pieces, but it isn't essential. Small pieces of canvas can be inserted into a larger frame by stitching the canvas to scrap fabric, carefully cutting away fabric behind the stitching area and then inserting the fabric into the frame as usual. However, all of these projects can be completed without a frame providing that you use a good rigid canvas and that you keep your tension light and even. Small projects such as cushions, pictures, mats etc are easily stitched without a frame – which make them good portable projects to keep in your bag for whiling away an idle moment.

Even if your eyesight is young and sound, because the projects are miniatures you may well find it easier to use a *magnifying glass* while working. An inventive array of magnifying implements have been designed specifically with craftworkers in mind: best of all is a combination magnifying light which spotlights your work as you stitch – very useful for evening work.

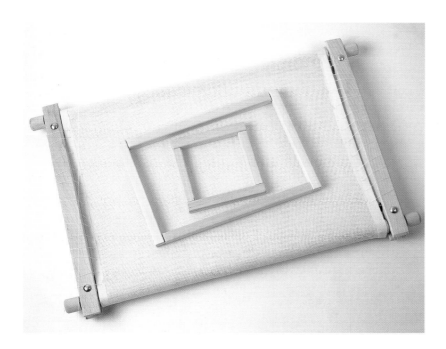

Basic Guide
to Stitching

Needlepoint is not difficult to do. If you're completely new to the idea, just take it slowly and practise on a little piece of canvas before you start your grand project.

Before you start

Find somewhere comfortable to sit – put your feet up if you can. It's best not to try watching TV at the same time as stitching: it's tiring for the eyes to be constantly re-focusing, and I confess to having made some Big-Time mistakes by working like this. Try to have a good light source above or slightly behind you, so that the light falls on your work and not in your eyes. Sunlight is best of all, and it makes you feel good too. Needlepoint is great therapy, so make sure that you enjoy it!

Select your project and, if you aren't using a frame, cut a piece of canvas to the size specified. You'll see that this size is a little larger than the finished dimensions given for the project, because extra canvas has been allowed for turnings (see Basic Guide to Finishing, page 16). Of course you can use a piece of canvas larger than the size quoted, but I wouldn't recommend going smaller as you might not have enough margin left.

Next, provide yourself with sufficient threads to complete your project. Cut a length of thread, about 50-60 cm long, from each colour specified in the project key. Stranded cottons are generally sold in 8-metre skeins, made up of six single strands of thread. For the fine 22 tpi canvas you will only need to use three of these strands in the needle to create a stitch of the right thickness, so your next task is to divide each cut length into two batches of three strands.

It's quite convenient to have a needle threaded up with each colour ready to be used when needed – like having a different paintbrush for each colour – so thread three strands into each needle and tie a small knot in the other end of the thread.

TIP
Cut threads 50-60 cm long.

Very long threads
– wear thin and go fluffy
– may tangle as you work
– make for more arm stretching

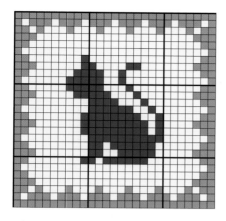

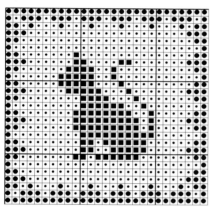

PROJECTS KEY		ANCHOR	DMC	MADEIRA
• Off white	275	746	0101
● Soft brown	914	407	2310
■ Dark brown	381	938	2006

The two charts on the left are for working the same project – the small cat cushion on page 33; the key for both charts is shown above. If you prefer working from a colour chart, follow the coloured blocks in the key to find which thread to use for which stitch. If you prefer working from a black and white chart (for instance, you might want to photocopy a chart to carry around with your stitching), follow the symbols given in the key to check which stitch is worked in which thread.

Reading the pattern

The pattern or chart consists of lots of lines forming squares: each square contains a colour (on the coloured charts) or a symbol (if you're working from the black and white charts). Each square represents a stitch, and each colour or symbol in that square tells you what colour thread to use for that stitch, guided by the key alongside the chart. Remember that the lines on the pattern do not represent the threads of your canvas, but each square on the pattern represents one stitch.

Sometimes you'll notice that the colours on the charts are slightly different from the actual thread colours they represent; this is because the differences between the colours on the charts are exaggerated to make them easy to read.

> REMEMBER:
> *each square on the pattern*
> *= one stitch on your canvas.*

Starting stitching

The needlepoint stitch is often called a tapestry stitch, but it has several other names too. If you decide to stitch diagonally across the canvas then it's called basketweave stitch, because that's the kind of pattern it creates on the back of your work. If you choose to stitch horizontally across the canvas it's referred to as petit point or tent stitch. I find the basketweave stitch easier to work, and it also helps to prevent the canvas from distorting, but do use whichever method you like best: there's no right or wrong here.

If you've never stitched before, I suggest that you cut a small piece of practice canvas. Push one of your ready-threaded needles through a hole in the canvas from the right side of your work through to the back and then bring it up again through another hole about one finger's width away from the first. This hole is the starting point for your first stitch (see figure a).

Fig a

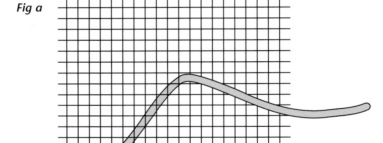

Fig b

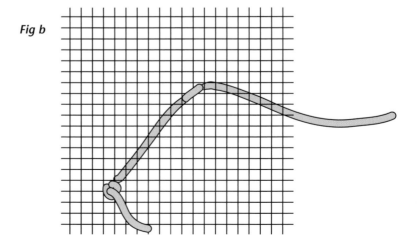

Now push the needle through to the back of the canvas again, using a hole diagonally above and to the right (see figure b). You have now made your first stitch! Don't worry about the knot – the thread lying under your canvas will be secured by subsequent stitches, and when you reach the knot it can then be safely cut off.

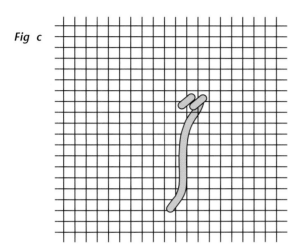

Fig c

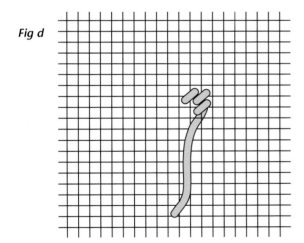

Fig d

For basketweave stitch you now make your next stitch beside the first stitch (figure c) and the following stitch below the second (figure d).

Fig e

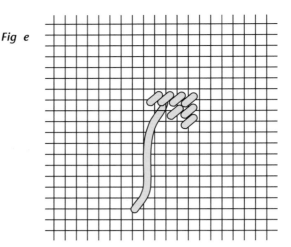

You then continue working diagonally across the canvas (figure e), bringing in other colours as required by the pattern. Remember to start them all off as described above, beginning from the right side, a finger's width from where you want that colour to start.

When you're close to the end of a length of thread, finish it off neatly by passing it through a few stitches on the back of your work.

You will save thread and achieve a flatter, neater job if you work all the same-coloured stitches in one area at the same time. Practise a few stitches to get the feel of it; you'll soon get into a rhythm.

Building up a design

This is fine for the background, I hear you cry, but what about the fiddly bits? Once again there are different ways of working, and there's no substitute for practice to find your own preferred method. What I usually do is start in the top right-hand corner of the pattern and work diagonally across the canvas until I get to more complicated sections; at this point I might stop and put in some detail, and then continue with the background. This does mean that I may have several different colours on the go at the same time and my work has threads and needles hanging from it for a time, but it all gets sorted out in the end.

If you prefer to work the main design motifs first and then fill in the background, ensure that you count your threads carefully, and double-check the chart before beginning to stitch any area. When working an intricate design, keep taking your bearings to check that you have not gone off course.

When you're working this teddy bear design you could begin with the bear itself and then stitch the background, or you could start with the routine stitching on the border and then work the teddy last. Either method works fine – it just depends which you prefer.

Although generally you start and finish threads by securing them under other stitches, you don't want to cover an end of a very dark thread with a pale colour as it may show through the finished work, so just be aware of this problem. For example, on the cat designs: because the background is pale and the cat is dark, try either stitching the background first, or make sure that you start and finish the dark thread underneath the brown cat.

When I was at school my teacher was forever turning over my feeble attempt at embroidery and criticizing its untidiness. Don't worry about the back of your work, as it won't be visible after completing your project – and you're no longer at school! However, do remember to cut off knots once the threads are secured to avoid making any bumps; these will show up as lumps on such small pieces of work.

It may sound glaringly obvious, but do keep your work clean – wash your hands before stitching, and keep the work covered when it's not in use. Your stitching represents many hours of work, and needs to be valued accordingly.

When you're working a design such as this one, with a dark motif on a light background, make sure that you begin your dark threads on a part of the canvas where they won't show through the paler areas of stitching.

Mistakes

Lastly – we all make mistakes. Many hand-made oriental carpets from Islamic countries traditionally contain small errors: apparently this is done deliberately by the weavers as a sign of humility – because 'only Allah is perfect.' It is, of course, a great excuse for an oversight, but if you do spot a recent mistake it's usually possible to undo the last few stitches and put the error right.

Do not be tempted to unpick with scissors, as you will probably cut right through the canvas and make an irreparable hole. There speaks the voice of experience. If just one or two stitches are the wrong colour and it's too late to undo them, then it's usually possible to overstitch them with the correct colour – pull the stitch down firmly so that it doesn't stand proud of its neighbours. If the whole thing is just a horrible mess and you cannot stand the sight of it, don't be ashamed to bin your project and put it down to experience. You're not alone: we've all done it.

Basic Guide to Finishing

Once your stitching is complete spend a few moments to check for missed stitches and to tidy up any loose threads. Flat projects are the easiest to deal with, so we'll start with them.

Mats, rugs and carpets

Look at your work to see if it's 'square' – that is, are the edges properly at right-angles? If it looks a bit skew-whiff, try pulling it gently back into shape. If it's badly distorted, dampen it very lightly (for instance with a fine spray from a water-bottle), then pin it back into shape on a board and leave it to dry. Make sure that you use rust-free pins for this process. Also, pressing the back of the work gently with a steam iron then pulling the piece into shape can sometimes do the trick.

The small bathmat above and the spectacular large carpet on the right are both finished off in exactly the same way – by pressing the raw edges to the back and securing them with fusible interfacing.

Trim any excess canvas to leave a border of about 1.5cm all around your stitching. Large carpets, such as the one in the drawing room (page 104), could take a wider border – perhaps 3cm. Fold this border to the back of the work, mitring the canvas at the corners, and lightly press from the wrong side with a warm iron.

To back your work, simply take a piece of iron-on fusible interfacing (Vilene or similar), cut it fractionally smaller than your stitched work, and iron it into place on the back of your work. This not only hides any untidiness on the wrong side, but also protects the work and provides what we all need – a good flat bottom.

Cushions

These are rather more fiddly than the flat items, but a little patience will work wonders. The conventional way to make a real-size cushion is to seam it on the wrong side then turn it right-side-out – and hey presto, there's a cushion. Don't even consider doing that with these tiny cushions: you will surely go insane.

All you need to do is trim the canvas to about 1cm all around your stitched work, and cut a piece of fabric to the same size (cotton is easiest to work with). Next, fold the canvas border to the wrong side of the work, mitring it at the corners. Fold a 1cm turning all around your fabric square, mitring the corners so that the finished panel is the same size as your stitched work. Now simply stitch them together, preferably using ladder stitch, leaving a hole in one side for the filling.

A small piece of toy-filling or cotton-wool can be used – resist the temptation to overstuff the cushion or it will look like a ball. Lastly, close up the opening. If you wish you can make a braid with spare threads then stitch or glue this around the edges.

When you're working on cushions this tiny, fold under the edges and stitch the cushion front to a matching piece of fabric; stuff the cushion gently before you close the final seam.

Pictures and samplers

Trim away any excess canvas to leave only a small border around your stitching, then lightly glue the border and stick the panel over a piece of card. It's possible to buy a wide variety of frames in miniature shops; sometimes you'll find a suitable frame which already contains a picture – this can generally be removed pretty easily and replaced with your own work. If your frame is too

deep you can cut a piece of thin card the same size as your picture to fill up the extra space; if the frame is too large in area, cut a surround for your stitching from paper or thin card in a toning or complementary colour.

Alternatively, you might consider making your own frame. You can 'do it yourself' using ready-made rebated moulding, or you can create your own frame from matchsticks or offcuts of wood. For unusual textures, glue little objects such as shells, rice or tiny dried pasta shapes onto a card or wood backing, then paint or gild them. Wherever possible, do your varnishing or painting before inserting your needlework, for obvious reasons.

Stools, chairs, settees and toyboxes

If you want to stitch a seat-cover for a ready-made piece of furniture, trace the seat shape as accurately as possible. From this tracing draw and cut a cardboard template of the seat shape; try it in the piece of furniture to check for accuracy. Lay the template on your canvas and, adding extra where necessary for turnings, lightly pencil the shape onto your canvas. This is the area you need to cover with needlework.

Count the stitches on the design you would like to use and see how this relates to the shape drawn on your canvas. If the pattern is larger than your drawn shape, then obviously you will lose part of the pattern; this might not matter very much if the outside of the design is relatively plain.

This dining chair was made up from a kit; you can get kits to suit different historical periods, or you can build your own furniture.

If your template is larger than the design, continue the pattern by adding more stitches until your pencil line is covered. Remember, though, to keep the design centred on your canvas; it's best to start in the middle and work outwards towards the edges.

The chair seats and settee top in this book are designed to fit House of Miniatures Chippendale furniture kits, but with a little fiddling you can probably make them fit your own ready-made furniture.

When you have finished your stitching, trim away any excess canvas, allowing a small margin (about 1.5 cm) around your work. Place the canvas over your cardboard template, fold the edges under, then glue them to the back of the template. When the glue is dry, insert the finished seat into your chair or settee, glueing it lightly in place if necessary.

The stools used in this book are ones that I bought ready-made but unfinished. These are supplied as a base with a separate top. If yours is the same, discard the top then stain or varnish the base as desired. Make up a template to fit the top, then cover it with your stitching as described above and glue it onto your stool base. You can then finish the edges of your work with wood moulding, braid, cord etc.

This stool was bought ready-made; I painted the base in a toning colour before I added the stitched top.

This toybox was bought as a blanket box; I simply added the stitched and padded top and finished it off with a little braid.

Basic Guide to Designing

Varying the basic projects

Maybe you have a fancy to stitch one of the patterns in this book but you just don't like my choice of colours – or perhaps they don't match the wallpaper or curtains in your dolls' house?

No problem. It's very simple just to substitute your own colour choices for the ones that I've given. Make a note of which threads you intend to substitute, and what you've changed them to, and do remember to maintain the contrasts – so, for instance, make sure that motifs stand out against the background. Unless you're going for a very jazzy look, avoid using the very bright shades; they're fine in your real home, but in miniature homes they rather tend to leap out at you. Even pure white should be used sparingly as it can look a bit too bright.

There are other ways, too, of customizing the designs I've given you; as well as varying the colours, you can change borders or add new ones. A border can be as simple as a single line of colour, or two lines of different colours. Experiment!

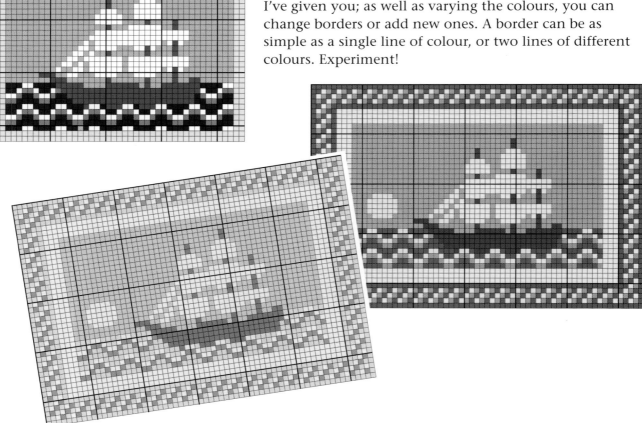

Don't be afraid to use one of the designs for a different project. For example: to make a matching chair seat for the nursery projects, just make a template of your chair seat as described in Basic Guide to Finishing (see page 18), and pencil the required stitched area onto your canvas. Stitch one of the teddies in the centre of your chair seat, then fill in the background with a plain contrasting colour.

Designing your own projects

If you complete all the projects in this book, you may be itching to start something new. If you can't wait for the next book, why not try designing some projects yourself? You'll find many sources of inspiration for your own designs. Patterns are everywhere you look – wallpapers, furnishings, clothes and even in nature – but remember that you can't use copyright designs if you intend to sell your work.

If you want your designs to fit in with a specific historical period or a particular theme, your local library can usually help out. Specialist books on carpets are few

My first rough sketch (below) for the galleon motif used in the bathroom projects.

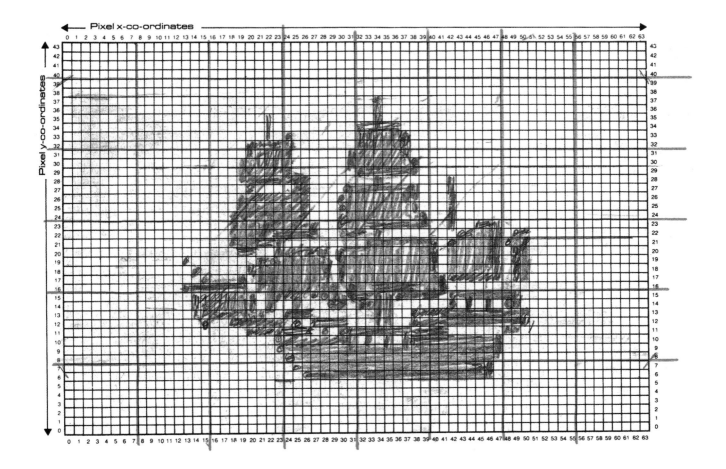

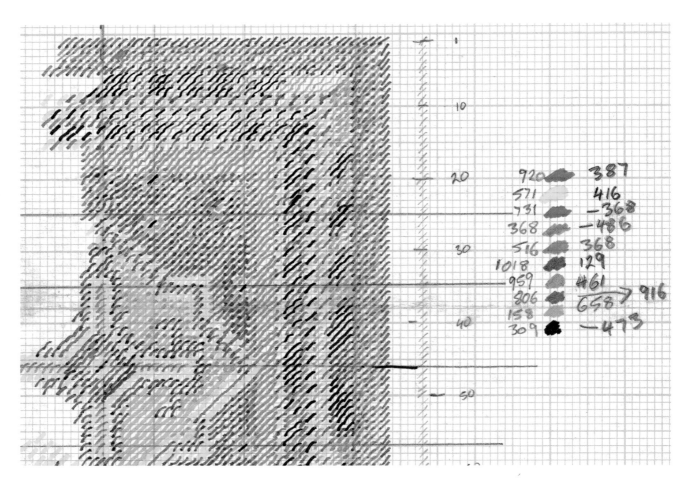

720 387
571 416
731 −368
368 −486
516 368
1018 129
959 461
806 658 ⟩ 916
158
309 −473

Virtually anything can be the inspiration for a needlepoint project, either simple or complex. The rough chart (above) shows my first colour jottings for a design based on the carpet (right). The little butterfly design (opposite) looked just right as the centrepiece of a flower garland.

and far between, but there are plenty of books on ceramics and furnishings to illustrate the popular designs of particular eras. Books about stately homes and their contents are also a rich source of ideas. Do your homework and get the feel of your period, but then be inventive and produce something fresh and original to make your dolls' house unique.

When you have some ideas for your design, sketch the basic shape of it onto a piece of paper. Next, take some graph paper and flesh out your sketch by colouring in the squares appropriately. Then try stitching a little piece of the design to see if it works. If you're starting with something very small – a cushion, for instance – then you can use larger squares (a child's squared maths book is ideal).

Also, we can't ignore the march of technology which has led to the development of a number of helpful computer programmes for creating your own designs. I use one by Ursa which provides a piece of graph paper on screen, a palette of colours and lots of useful little tricks to make life easier for the designer. However, I do believe that you need to know the basic principles of design before asking a computer to help you, so I suggest trying the graph paper method first.

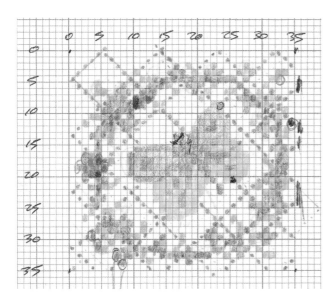

These examples show the progression of a design from my first rough drawing (right). I've then refined the design on the computer and produced symbol and colour versions of the chart (below). In the photograph (opposite), the finished, stitched item is shown in its room setting. The lighthouse has come a long way from my initial sketch!

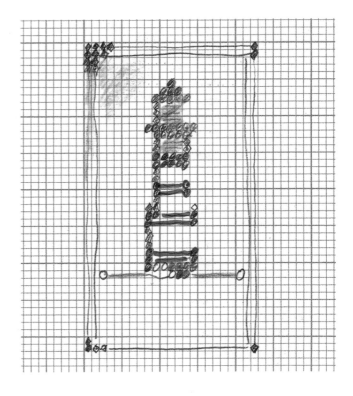

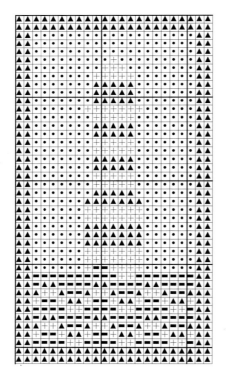

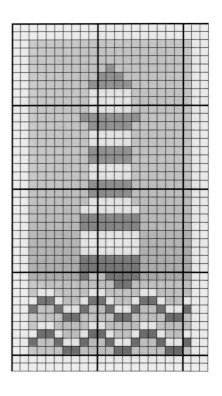

Notes on working the projects in this book

In the Basic Guides section I've covered all the technical know-how you need for producing successful projects; the following notes are useful additional guidelines which will help you as you work your way through the projects.

- All measurements are given in metric, and thread quantities are provided in metres or parts of a metre. So, 3m means three metres, and 2.5m means two and a half metres. If you prefer to work in imperial, you will find a conversion chart on page 112.

- Although 1/12th scale is the inch to a foot scale, I've used centimetres when giving measurements for the projects. This is because it's easier to give small measurements accurately in centimetres as they are smaller units than inches – it avoids all those eighths and sixteenths. Once again, though, if you would find it helpful to know the imperial equivalents, the conversion chart on page 112 will help you.

- At the beginning of each chapter there is a photograph of a room setting, showing all or most of the projects featured in that section. You will also find a complete list of the projects at the beginning of each chapter.

- Under the heading 'You will need:' you will find the thread and canvas quantities for each project listed individually. Under 'finished sizes' you will find the approximate size of each project when you have stitched it: if you add anything to your design, such as an extra border or a frame, then this will increase the finished size.

- The canvas sizes I've given are quite generous, so that there is plenty of spare canvas around the stitching to allow for finishing. However, if you have any scraps of canvas left over from other bits of stitching you may well be able to use them up on the smaller projects – just check the finished size of the project and make sure that you leave a margin of at least 1.5cm all around the work – preferably more.

- If you're stitching several projects, then of course they can all be worked on one large piece of canvas; this is especially useful if you're using a frame – but again, do remember to leave plenty of space between the projects.

- The thread quantities given are also generous, but some people use their thread in an economical way while others are quite profligate! If you want to add extra border colour, or to use the same-coloured thread to stitch up a cushion, then remember that you may require extra thread.

- For simplicity, the minimum quantity of thread I've given for any colour is one metre, but obviously if you plan to stitch more than one project you may well save on the total amount of thread required.

TAKE ONE CAT . . .

TAKE ONE CAT...

ROOM:

entrance hall

PROJECTS:

cushion
doormat
sampler

DIFFICULTY RATING:

beginner

Did you know that the scientist Sir Isaac Newton is credited with inventing the cat flap for the use of his own cats?

If you have a very grand dolls' house then doubtless you'll also have a very grand entrance hall to go with it – and I, for one, am very envious! However, for most of us the hallway of a dolls' house is just a narrow space which accommodates the stairwell and the front door. For this reason it's often an overlooked area, receiving minimum attention while the full force of our decorative imagination is directed at the main rooms of the house. But, just as in a real-size home, first impressions count. So why not give your hall a coordinated look? These three small projects can be used to enhance the smallest of spaces. After all, you must have room for a doormat – and surely the sampler could hang on the wall by the stairs? And I bet you have space too for a simple chair to hold the cushion.

So now you've not only introduced a theme to your entrance hall but also established a good character reference for the residents; if they are cat lovers, then they must be very pleasant people. In my experience many miniaturists are also cat lovers, just as many cats are dolls' house enthusiasts ... my three cats are always keen to explore a new house or rearrange furniture, especially those nice little dangly lights.

Many modern houses and apartments have an extremely small entrance hall, sometimes no more than a vestibule – somewhere to put wet umbrellas and muddy boots. It's almost as if this area is being squeezed out of the home – and yet many centuries ago a house was little more than just a very large hall. Our English word 'hall' itself is derived from the Old English 'heall,' which simply meant 'shelter' – a place for sheltering from the weather, and an empty space in which to eat and sleep.

Slowly houses evolved which had separate chambers off the large central hall, and eventually these separate chambers themselves became the important rooms. With the advent of smaller homes in recent years no large communal hall is necessary, and the hall has dwindled in importance to a place you pass through before you enter the main rooms of a house. In humbler homes the hall has been reduced to a mere corridor, not a place in which you are intended to spend any significant time.

The aim of this project is to add interest and character to the hallway, without detracting from the overall colour schemes of the more important rooms in the house. To achieve this, and to make the appeal of the designs as universal as possible, I've used natural colours which will tone in well with the wooden features often found in halls – stair spindles, door architrave, panelling etc.

As these are the first projects in the book, they are aimed specifically at the beginner; even if you're completely new to needlepoint, you should be able to stitch all of these items very easily. And the projects in this section are all very small items, so even if you do make a mistake and have to unpick a bit or start again, you won't have lost too much time!

If you've mastered the basics of stitching and are interested in moving on to design, these projects demonstrate how simple it can be to customize your own needlework designs and create coordinating patterns. I began with a simple and recognisable one-colour motif – the cat. Then I added a plain background. It's helpful to have a good contrast between your main motif and the background colour.

Lettering was then added – 'welcome' – for the door mat. (If you prefer it could be 'beware'! Or even be the family name for that personal touch.) Finally I added a border, which again uses just one colour, in a pattern which is very simple and easy to follow but also very effective. It's one of the bonuses of miniature needlework, that a design which would look very plain in a real-size rug looks just right when it's been condensed down to 1/12th scale.

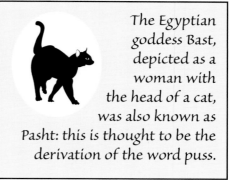

The Egyptian goddess Bast, depicted as a woman with the head of a cat, was also known as Pasht: this is thought to be the derivation of the word puss.

You will need

For each project you will need size 26 needles, plus canvas and threads as listed below. Thread quantities are approximate and you may well need less, but allow an extra piece of the soft brown if you wish to use that colour to stitch up the finished cushion. (Alternatively, if you have a piece of canvas 10 x 30cm and buy an 8m skein of each thread colour, you will have sufficient to create all three projects with threads to spare.)

PROJECT	22tpi canvas	THREAD LENGTHS PER COLOUR			Finished size
		Off white	Soft brown	Dark brown	
doormat	12 x 10cm	3m	1.5m	1m	6.2 x 4cm
sampler	10 x 10cm	2m	1m	1m	5 x 2.7cm
cushion	10 x 10cm	1.5m	1m	1m	3.1 x 3.1cm
• For imperial measurements please refer to the conversion chart on page 112 •					

How to work the projects

For all the projects, follow the basic stitching instructions given in Basic Guides. If you're a complete beginner, you might find it helpful to stitch the borders first, to ensure that you've stitched the pattern correctly; you can then add the motif and finally fill in the background.

Doormat

Cushion

PROJECTS KEY		ANCHOR	DMC	MADEIRA
▫ •	Off white	275	746	0101
▨ ●	Soft brown	914	407	2310
■ ■	Dark brown	381	938	2006

Charts for doormat

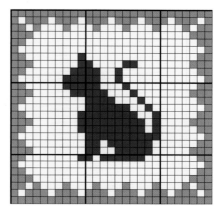

Charts for cushion

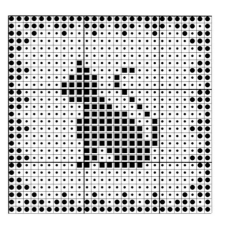

PROJECTS KEY	ANCHOR	DMC	MADEIRA
• Off white	275	746	0101
● Soft brown	914	407	2310
■ Dark brown	381	938	2006

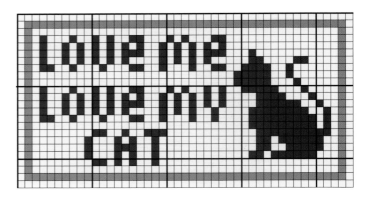

Charts for sampler

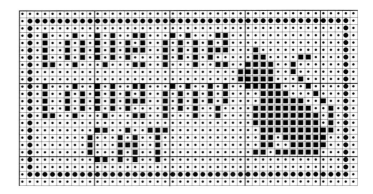

Making up

For finishing the cushion and mat see the Basic Guide to Finishing (page 16); you'll need a small piece of fusible interfacing for the mat, and fabric and stuffing for the cushion. The sampler was framed by Harry, my useful husband: if you don't have a Harry who can do the task, you might be able to find a small frame in a shop. If the frame is too big, try adding a card insert to fill up the space. You could also make your own frame out of miniature mouldings or even from strips of braid or lace.

Alternatively, you could simply trim the canvas to about 1cm all round, glue it to a piece of card the same size as your finished stitching (5 x 2.7cm), then fold the spare canvas under and glue it to the back of the card. With this method the border of your stitching creates its own frame.

Variations

If you want to make your doormat larger, simply increase the width of the outer borders – for example, make the cream band 4 stitches wide and the outer brown band also 4 stitches wide. This would add another 6 stitches to

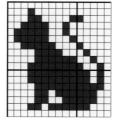

each side, which means that your mat will be roughly half an inch bigger in each dimension.

You can easily vary the colours on these designs. Any other colour will do for the background – just make sure that it contrasts with the browns. Try another pastel colour – pale pink, blue, peach. Of course you can also change the motif colour – after all, cats come in many colours. Try the lovely Siamese cats below on a blue or green background, or a traditional black and white tom cat. A ginger cat can be achieved by using three strands of different colours (orange/tan/white) in the same needle. Get inventive and try to match the colours of your own cat!

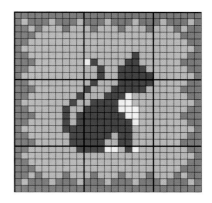

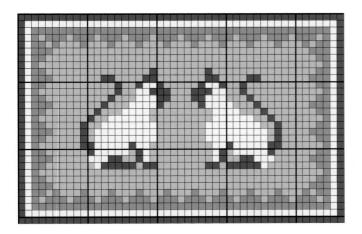

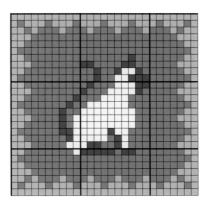

ALL AT SEA . . . .

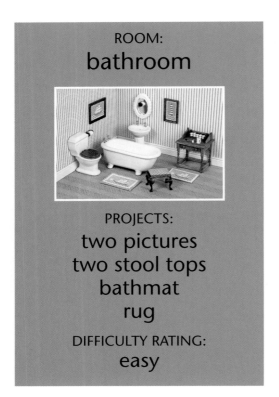

ROOM:
bathroom

PROJECTS:

two pictures
two stool tops
bathmat
rug

DIFFICULTY RATING:

easy

It's said of King James I that he was washed only twice in his life – at his birth and at his death – and that they had to cut off his vest when he died!

CHAPTER 2
ALL AT SEA...

Ancient Romans were undoubtedly a clean lot, and tended to build bath-houses in the countries they conquered. After the fall of the Roman Empire they left behind many useful things as they retreated back to the Mediterranean, but the practice of bathing was not one of them. For some reason it just didn't catch on – maybe bathing in colder climes wasn't such fun without the Romans' underfloor heating?

After a lull of several hundred years, crusaders returning from the Muslim east brought the custom of bathing to western countries. But alas, yet again it didn't catch on in a big way, and the Middle Ages must have been pretty unpleasant even if you managed to survive all those wars, rebellions and plagues.

As towns developed, people found it difficult and expensive to get drinking water to their homes, so naturally they weren't going to waste it by sprinkling it on their bodies. And no doubt so many people living in such close proximity led to the fashion for building bath-houses in many cities. Elizabethan London had public bath-houses called Hummums, which may have been the origin of the phrase 'to hum,' meaning to smell.

In 18th-century Europe bathing was associated with the fashionable study of all things Greek and Roman, and finally caught on – although only among the upper classes. Bathing out of doors was quite the thing.

During the 19th century, plumbing made great strides; although plumbed-in bathrooms, with hot and cold water on tap, were rare before the middle of the century, by the end a large country house could be expected to have a number of bathrooms. There could be, though, a snobbery element to not having a bathroom; Oscar Wilde complained about having wash-basins in rooms at the Savoy Hotel, London: 'after all, if you wanted hot water to wash in, you could always ring and have the maid bring it.'

A bathroom inside every home is just about universal today, but I'm sure that there are many of us who can still remember being bathed in front of the fire or having to go to an outhouse.

In real life our bathrooms are often tucked into small spaces in our homes, crowded with essential equipment and with hardly room to swing the proverbial cat. However, in our make-believe world we find that many dolls' houses don't even come with a small room intended as a bathroom, which means sacrificing one of the bedrooms for the purpose. In this case you end up with quite a large room to fill, but don't despair; it's really easy to find suitable furnishings these days. There are plenty of bathroom accessories available – plain bathroom suites, decorated ones, corner baths, shower cabinets, towel rails, cabinets and much more.

Whether your bathroom is large or small, you can make it different from the rest by giving it a 'theme;' here I've chosen a nautical motif. Britain, my home country, has always had close links with the sea and the seaside theme is much beloved, especially in coastal resorts. So let yourself go and create an exciting bathroom.

William Weddell, the patron of Robert Adam, bathed in an Egyptian sarcophagus. Now there's a theme for a miniature bathroom!

Ship bathmat To create a bathmat like this one, use just the centre of the chart given for the main rug (see page 43).

You will need

For each project you will need size 26 needles, plus canvas and threads as listed below. Thread quantities are approximate and you may well need less.

PROJECT	22tpi canvas	THREAD LENGTHS PER COLOUR					Finished size
		Dark cream	Brown	Blue	Dark blue	Grey	
rug	13 x 11cm	3m	1m	2.5m	1.5m	2.5m	7.3 x 5.1cm
bathmat	12 x 10cm	2.5m	1m	2.5m	1m	1.5m	6.3 x 4.1cm
stool top 1	10 x 10cm	1m	1m	2m	–	–	4 x 2.8cm
stool top 2	10 x 10cm	1m	–	–	1m	2m	4 x 2.8cm
picture 1	10 x 10cm	2m	1m	2m	1m	1m	5 x 3.7cm
picture 2	10 x 10cm	1.5m	–	1.5m	1m	1m	4.7 x 2.6cm
• For imperial measurements please refer to the conversion chart on page 112 •							

How to work the projects

These projects are all straightforward to stitch. The ship may look complicated, but if you just start with the sails and then do the brown thread it will soon come together; follow the basic stitching instructions given on page 10. Never be afraid of something that looks complicated – just allow yourself time to take it slowly. Please do note, though, that the ship used for the stool top is smaller than the ship used for the other designs.

No separate pattern is given for the bathmat; simply use the pattern for the rug, but ignore the striped border – i.e., start four stitches in from each edge.

Charts for stool top 1

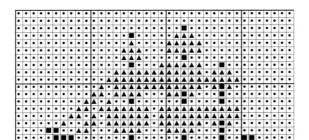

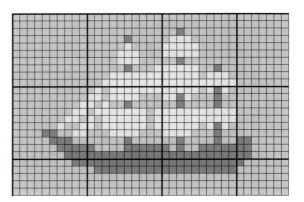

Picture 1

Stool top 1

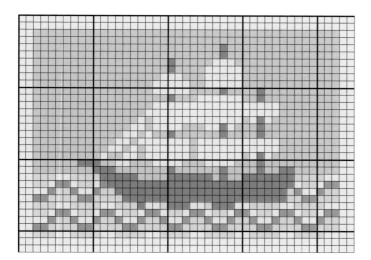

PROJECTS KEY		ANCHOR	DMC	MADEIRA
▲	Dark cream	386	746	2512
■	Brown	914	407	2310
•	Blue	120	794	0909
+	Dark blue	121	809	0906
–	Grey	847	928	1805

Charts for picture 1

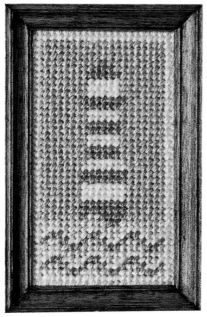

Picture 2

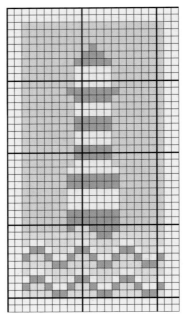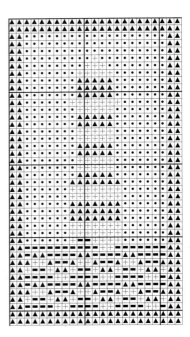

Charts for picture 2

Stool top 2

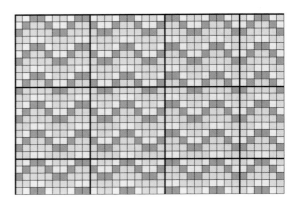

Charts for stool top 2

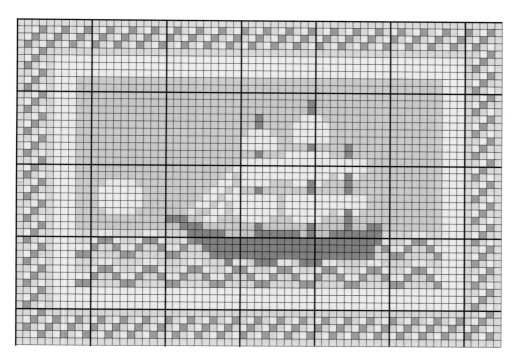

Charts for rug

PROJECTS KEY		Anchor	DMC	Madeira
▲	Dark cream	386	746	2512
■	Brown	914	407	2310
•	Blue	120	794	0909
+	Dark blue	121	809	0906
▬	Grey	847	928	1805

Rug

TIP

Make your project larger by adding extra rows of border – use wide bands of one colour to keep it simple.

Making up

For finishing all these items see the Basic Guide to Finishing (page 16). You will need a small piece of fusible interfacing to back the rug and the bathmat, and either ready-made or DIY stools and picture frames. If you don't have a stool and the thought of making one is too daunting, why not try making a simple storage chest (just flat pieces of wood held together by gluing them to small blocks inside); you can then trim and glue your needle-work to the top, finishing with a fine braid to cover the edges. Add brass handles and a lock, and it could even be an old sea chest.

Variations

The colours here have been kept deliberately cool, reminiscent of wintry seas with a cold watery sun close to the horizon; these shades will tone well with plain cream or even wood-panelled bathroom fixtures. However, if you really want to make a splash in your bathroom, warm up the colours by using mediterranean hues: deep blues and turquoises, a bright red ship and a yellow sun. Use lots of white on the walls in your bathroom so that the whole thing really stands out.

The nautical idea can work just as well in a little boy's bedroom or even an old sea captain's study, and an alternative green/red colourway (right) would create a markedly different effect by using stronger, more 'masculine' colours. Or you could try primary colours (below) for an infant's room.

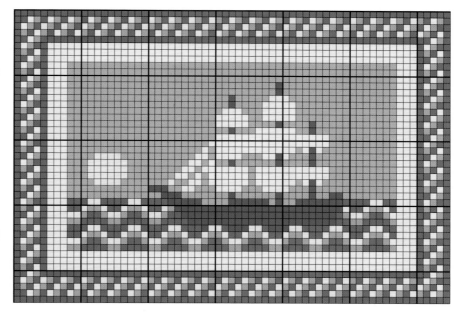

Just a few nautical elements have been picked out for these designs – the sea, a ship and a lighthouse – but what about using tiny shells as a wall decoration or as a soap dish? Use a piece of 'rope' (braid) looped around the sides of the bath or as a dado. The net bags that hold fruit make ideal fish-net which could be draped over a curtain rail, and model ship shops sell wonderful little things such as lifebelts and ships' wheels which can be added as decoration. I'd suggest plain colour-washed walls, but you could add a stencil or a cut-out border of shells, starfish etc. Miniaturists are such resourceful people that I'm sure you'll be able to come up with lots of other ideas.

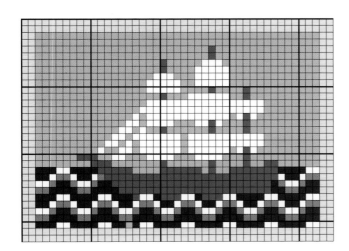

TEDDY BEARS' PICNIC . . . .

CHAPTER 3

TEDDY BEARS' PICNIC...

ROOM:

nursery

PROJECTS:

carpet
rug
toybox top
picture
two cushions

DIFFICULTY RATING:

easy/intermediate

Don't you envy children today, with their wonderful techno-toys, computer games, bright comfortable clothing and all those wonderful opportunities? Surely kids have never had it so good? Maybe so, but perhaps too they're making up for many lost childhoods from the past. Childhood hasn't always been the unending fun it seems to be nowadays.

Before the early decades of this century many children died before reaching adulthood, but even for those who survived, childhood was very short indeed. Once past the toddler stage children were expected to join in with adult life: a poor family would need its children to work alongside them, in fields or workshops, and a wealthy family would expect the girls to learn to sew and spin and learn the household arts, while boys would learn to ride and hunt. In the 18th century the first commercially-produced books for children appeared, and by the end of that century there was also a wide variety of puzzles and games – but these were not so much for the children's entertainment as for their education.

In large properties children were generally housed on the upper floors in rooms furnished with discarded items from the rest of the house. By the late 19th century an affluent home in Europe or America might include a nursery, night nursery and school-room. All the children would live together, eating, sleeping and learning in close proximity, cared for by a variety of servants.

During the 19th century special plain furniture evolved for nursery use, to go alongside the cast-offs from downstairs. It's hard to know whether this was driven by safety concerns (smoother furniture isn't so painful if you bump into it), or by economy (why spend lots on chairs and tables which will be subjected to hard use?). Simple high chairs – smaller chairs with very long legs – had been around for some time, but by the end of the century the specialized high chair was a common feature in nurseries, as were the brass and iron dropside cot and high wire-mesh guards for the open fires.

The industrial revolution brought a greater variety of toys to families that could afford them, and some of these toys were mechanized. Noah's Arks were popular toys, as were traditional role-play toys such as dolls, dolls' houses, prams and toy farms. Despite the greater prevalence of toys, kids were not necessarily having more fun, as they were often subjected to rigid discipline and their behaviour was judged by adult standards.

However by the end of the 19th century attitudes began to relax. Books on child psychology began to appear from Europe; children were beginning to be recognized as something special and different. They were no longer seen just as little adults, and childhood was extended so that you didn't have to leap straight from the nursery to adulthood. Small boys were dressed in knickerbockers or short trousers instead of frocks and petticoats; clothes for small girls became simpler and more practical; older children were given separate bedrooms apart from the nursery. The increased production of commercial toys led to a wide variety of readily-available and affordable playthings; at this stage the nursery came into its own as a truly child-friendly setting.

For my nursery designs I have chosen to use the teddy bear, partly because he appeals to both sexes and so will fit in with any nursery setting, but mostly because he's just cute. The teddy bear as we know him today wouldn't have appeared in a nursery before about 1906, but if you want to put a teddy in your Regency house, why not?

In 1902 Theodore (Teddy) Roosevelt chose not to shoot a bear during a hunting trip; this gave birth to a cartoon in the 'Washington Post' about Teddy's bear. Soon afterwards a bear appeared in a New York shop window carrying the name 'Teddy's Bear'. This title soon became just plain old teddy bear – and the shop owner went on to found the famous Ideal Toy Company.

You will need

For each project you will need size 26 needles, plus canvas and threads as listed below. Thread quantities are approximate and you may well need less, but allow an extra piece of blue if you wish to use it to stitch up the finished cushions.

Canvas sizes are approximate, so if you wish to use up odd pieces of canvas then check the finished sizes given – but do remember to leave a margin around your work for turnings.

PROJECT	22tpi canvas	THREAD LENGTHS PER COLOUR								Finished size
		Tan	Dark cream	Gold	Dark brown	Orange	Green	Blue	White	
carpet	20 x 17cm	1m	8.5m	3.5m	1m	1m	2.5m	10m	1m	11.5 x 9.5cm
rug	17 x 14cm	1m	5m	2.5m	1m	1m	1.5m	5m	–	9 x 6.8cm
toybox top	15 x 11cm	1m	3.5m	1.5m	1m	1m	1.5m	2.5m	–	8.4 x 4.4cm
picture	12 x 9cm	1m	2.5m	1m	1m	1m	1m	1.5m	–	6.5 x 4cm
sq. cushion	10 x 10cm	1m	1.5m	1m	1m	1m	–	1m	–	3.1 x 3.1cm
long cushion	10 x 10cm	1m	1.5m	1m	1m	1m	1m	1.5m	–	4.3 x 3.1cm

• For imperial measurements please refer to the conversion chart on page 112 •

Square cushion

How to work the projects

This chapter has a dual rating of easy/intermediate because some projects are simpler than others. For all the projects, follow the stitching instructions given in the Basic Guide to Stitching (see page 10). The carpet is the largest project that we've had so far, so if you're a beginner it may look daunting, but the stitching itself isn't complicated – it will just take a bit longer than the other projects in the section. Start with one of the smaller items such as a cushion, and work your way up to the others; by this stage you'll be familiar with the shape of the teddy and the flowers etc. When you come to the carpet, you might find it helpful to stitch the border framework first before starting on the central bears panel.

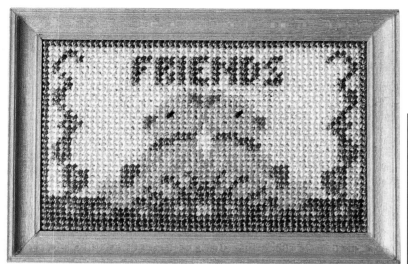

Picture

PROJECTS KEY	ANCHOR	DMC	MADEIRA
• Dark cream	300	677	2207
■ Gold	311	725	2513
○ Orange	1002	977	2301
∣ Tan	349	301	2306
+ Dark brown	381	938	2006
− Green	215	320	1310
▲ Blue	130	809	0910

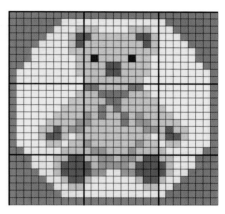

Above & below:
charts for square cushion

Charts for picture

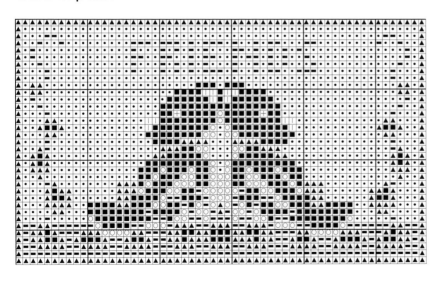

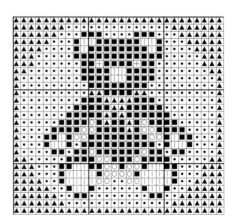

Rug

**Colour chart
for rug**

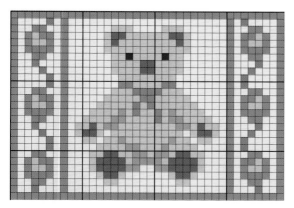

Charts for long cushion

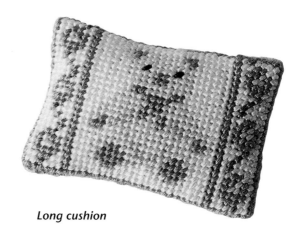

Long cushion

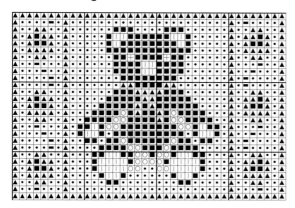

PROJECTS KEY		ANCHOR	DMC	MADEIRA
•	Dark cream	300	677	2207
■	Gold	311	725	2513
○	Orange	1002	977	2301
ǀ	Tan	349	301	2306
+	Dark brown	381	938	2006
–	Green	215	320	1310
▲	Blue	130	809	0910

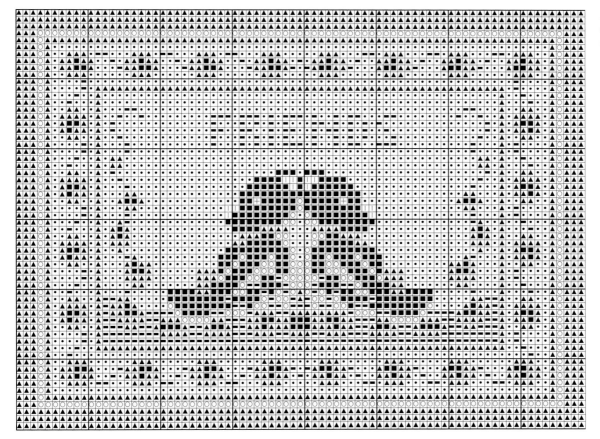

Symbols chart for rug

**Charts for
toybox top**

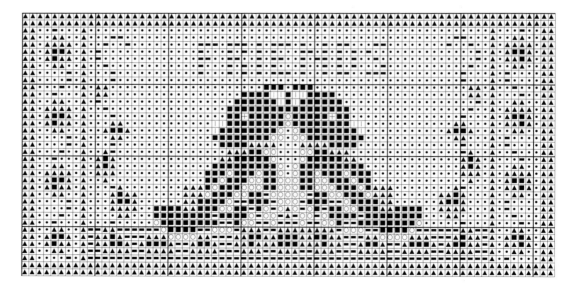

Carpet

PROJECTS KEY	ANCHOR	DMC	MADEIRA
• Dark cream	300	677	2207
■ Gold	311	725	2513
○ Orange	1002	977	2301
	Tan	349	301	2306
+ Dark brown	381	938	2006
- Green	215	320	1310
▲ Blue	130	809	0910
\ White	2	blanc	2402

Colour chart for carpet

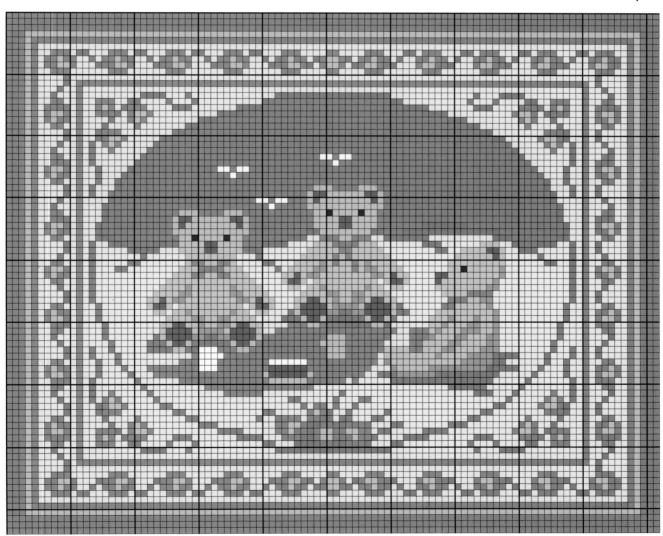

Symbols chart for carpet

PROJECTS KEY		Anchor	DMC	Madeira
	• Dark cream	300	677	2207
	■ Gold	311	725	2513
	○ Orange	1002	977	2301
	❘ Tan	349	301	2306
	+ Dark brown	381	938	2006
	▬ Green	215	320	1310
	▲ Blue	130	809	0910
	╲ White	2	blanc	2402

Making up

For finishing all these items see the Basic Guide to Finishing (page 16) for detailed advice; you will need fusible interfacing to back the carpet and rug, plus backing fabric and stuffing for the cushions, and you will also need either to make or to buy a toybox. The toybox shown here is actually sold as a blanket box. After the stitching was completed, I simply trimmed the canvas to about 1.5 cm outside the stitched area and folded it under, mitring the canvas at the corners. I used a small piece of felt to pad the centre of the design (you could use wadding or sponge instead if you prefer); I then glued the edges of the work, wrong side down, to the top of the box, and glued a matching trim round the edges to finish it off.

Variations

The toybox top could also be stitched as another small rug, or you could use it on items such as a built-in window seat or a long low footstool. Similarly, the long cushion design could also be a stool top, and the picture design could be a little rug. The designs are basically just rectangles of stitching – make them be what you want them to be!

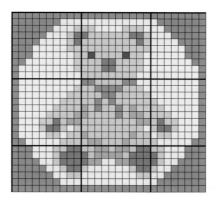

If you would prefer a different-coloured nursery, then it's a simple matter to exchange the blue for a pink, mid green, or rich peach. One word of warning – certain shades of pink and yellow can look a little sickly together, so pick a deep pink. Alternatively you could break away from the 'pastel' nursery look; these designs also look very bright and appealing with red flowers and borders.

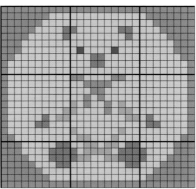

Chapter 4
BEDROOM

AND SO TO BED . . . .

CHAPTER 4

AND SO TO BED...

ROOM:
bedroom

PROJECTS:
carpet
stool top
three cushions

DIFFICULTY RATING:
intermediate

Cardinal Wolsey's Hampton Court Palace in England was provided with 280 beds but only 5 chairs!

The idea of having a home without a bedroom doesn't bear thinking about today, but in early mediaeval Europe all life was lived in one communal hall. As building constructions improved, a separate mezzanine chamber was created for the local lord or feudal overseer and his lady; this was by no means the bedroom that we know today, and it would probably have been shared with children and personal servants. The sleeping platform would have been bare boards, with an arrangement of curtains to provide privacy and added warmth for its occupants.

A description of a 12th-century English bed lists a ceiling canopy to keep out spiders, a feather mattress, muslin sheets and a coverlet of coarse wool lined with badger, beaver or cat. Personally I prefer my cats on top of the covers and alive, but the anti-spider device sounds like a great idea. This description obviously refers to the bed of a wealthy lord. A wooden truckle, which could be slid under the lord's bed during the day, came into use so that a servant could be at hand to protect and serve his master at all times. Most of the household would have had to make do with a mattress or pallet stuffed with straw, while others would have had no bed at all.

Gradually, further separate chambers were added to the houses of well-off people for guests, other family members and important servants. By now the sleeping apartment of the householder had become more of a bed-sitting room, and after dinner in the main hall, the master and his lady would withdraw to this room for the evening, perhaps with family or special guests. It was often known as a withdrawing chamber. The lady of the house would also use this room during the day to sew, spin and gossip with her ladies away from the bustle of the hall.

By the 16th century larger houses were furnished better, although still somewhat sparsely. The sleeping apartment would probably contain chests for storing valuables and clothing but little else. A bed, therefore was a valued piece of furniture. At this time the word 'bed' was applied to the mattress only; the framework on which it was placed was the bedstead.

Separate canopies over the bed had now given way to a natty all-in-one construction with a framework which would also support the curtains and a headboard. Sometimes the headboards could also be fitted out with little recesses for candles – presumably so that you could read in bed if you were rich and lucky enough to own a book, although it must have been a pretty dangerous enterprise with a straw mattress. A mattress filled with feathers was extremely expensive and for this reason would have been much prized.

By the middle of the 16th century we find the word 'bedchamber' in common use, the bed having been moved into a separate room off the withdrawing chamber which in turn now became a sort of private sitting room. This room eventually became the rather grander 'drawing room' in the English language.

In France it was customary for royalty to receive visitors and hold court while still abed, although there was often a little railing between the bed and the rest of the room – this was perhaps to prevent any over-familiarity, such as sitting on the end of the royal bed. Charles II, who spent much of his youth in France, brought this fashion back to England and it became very modish for a lady of fashion to receive guests of either sex in her bedroom while breakfasting in a state of dishabillé, or even while dressing for a ball or grand dinner.

By the end of the 18th century there was a wide variety of different types of furniture available (if you were rich), created by master cabinetmakers. As bedrooms had now become just sleeping chambers, so the furnishings became more functional. There was now room to add dressing tables, chairs and a clothes press (this was a cupboard with shelves and drawers in which the clothes were laid out). The cheval mirror was a popular addition to a Regency bedroom, and by the 1850s the brass bedstead had become popular among people who were well off. In large houses separate dressing rooms were added onto the main bedrooms – and eventually, of course, came the bathroom as part of the master-bedroom suite.

Shakespeare bequeathed his second-best bed to his widow and although this may sound paltry – if not downright insulting – to us, no doubt she was pleased to have it.

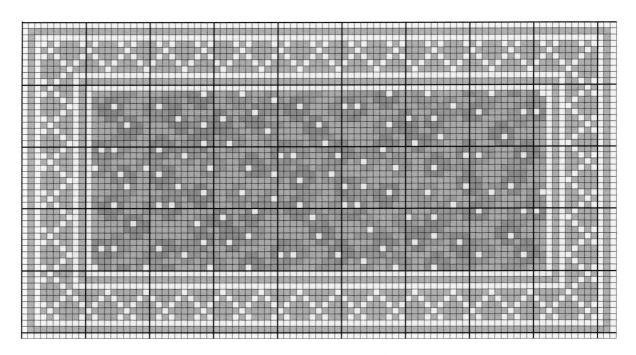

The chart above shows a variation on the basic carpet design shown on page 66; in this version the pansies fill the main panel of the carpet, with a geometric border.

Today our bedrooms are very much our own personal rooms, especially when they also act as dens, hideaways or studies for children, teenagers and students. Our own bedrooms express our personalities, perhaps more than any other room in the house. My bedroom is a sanctuary – a room I like to keep tidy and pleasant so that at any time I may retreat there to read, think or rest: a place of peace and tranquillity.

So, these designs have such a room in mind. The pink and blue pansies, set with a green and cream trellis framework in soft hues, help to create a pretty, cosy room. To suggest different types of personality for your bedroom's occupant you could perhaps add an armchair or a writing desk, or some pretty china and delicate pictures.

You will need

For each project you will need size 26 needles, plus canvas and threads as listed below. Thread quantities are approximate and you may well need less, but allow an extra piece of green if you wish to use it to stitch up the finished cushions.

Canvas sizes are approximate, so if you wish to use up odd pieces of canvas then check the finished sizes given – but do remember to leave a margin around your work for turnings.

PROJECT	22tpi canvas	THREAD LENGTHS PER COLOUR				Finished size
		Off white	Pale green	Lilac	Dark blue	
carpet	17 x 12cm	5m	7m	1.5m	1.5m	10.5 x 5.8cm
stool top	10 x 10cm	1m	2.5m	–	–	4.1 x 3.8cm
long cushion	10 x 10cm	1.5m	2m	1m	1m	4 x 3cm
cushion 1	10 x 10cm	1.5m	1.5m	–	–	3.1 x 3.1cm
cushion 2	10 x 10cm	1m	1.5m	1m	1m	3.1 x 3.1cm

• For imperial measurements please refer to the conversion chart on page 112 •

How to work the projects

All the stitching is straightforward; simply follow the stitching instructions given in the Basic Guide to Stitching (see page 10). If you're a beginner you might find it helpful to stitch the green and cream outlines first. The flowers are irregular, so don't worry if you misplace a few stitches – just as long as the shapes still look like flowers!

PROJECTS KEY		ANCHOR	DMC	MADEIRA
•	Off white	275	746	0101
▲	Pale green	875	503	1702
■	Lilac	96	554	2713
○	Dark blue	121	809	0906

Charts for cushion 1

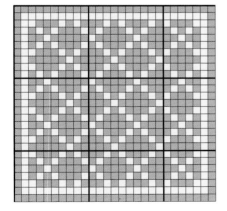
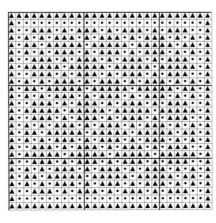

Cushion 1

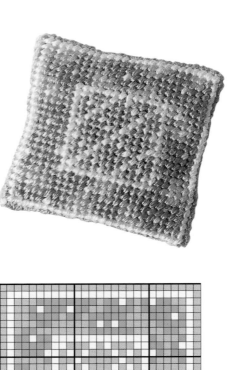

*Cushion 2 and
long cushion*

Charts for cushion 2

Charts for long cushion

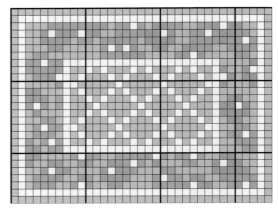

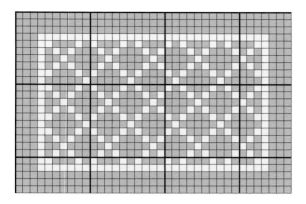

Charts for stool top

Stool top

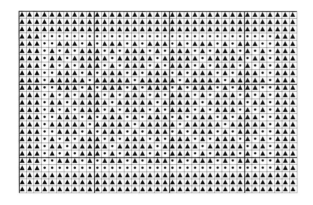

PROJECTS KEY		ANCHOR	DMC	MADEIRA
•	Off white	275	746	0101
▲	Pale green	875	503	1702
■	Lilac	96	554	2713
○	Dark blue	121	809	0906

Colour chart for carpet

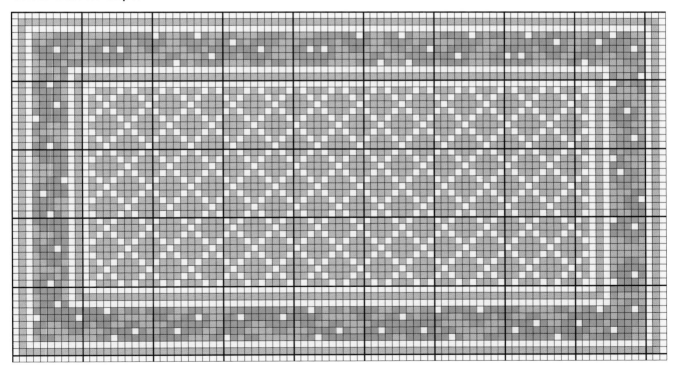

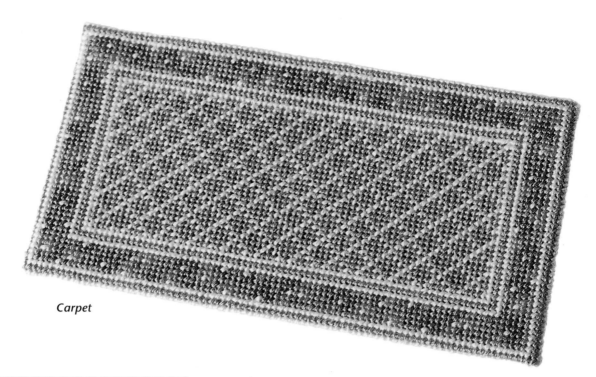

Carpet

PROJECTS KEY		ANCHOR	DMC	MADEIRA
•	Off white	275	746	0101
▲	Pale green	875	503	1702
■	Lilac	96	554	2713
○	Dark blue	121	809	0906

Making up

For finishing all these items see the Basic Guide to Finishing (page 16). You will need a small piece of fusible interfacing to back the carpet, and backing fabric and stuffing for the cushions. You will also need either to make or to buy a stool to suit the stool top.

Symbols chart for carpet

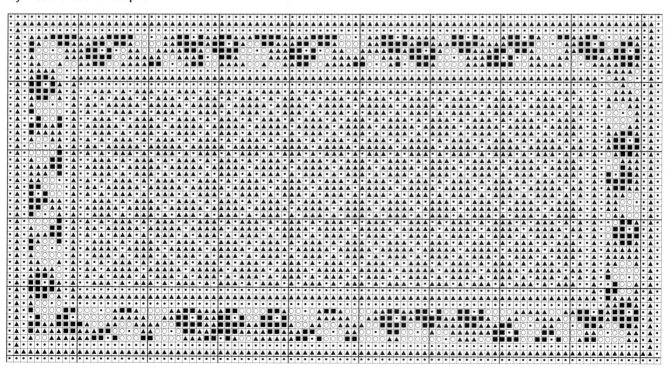

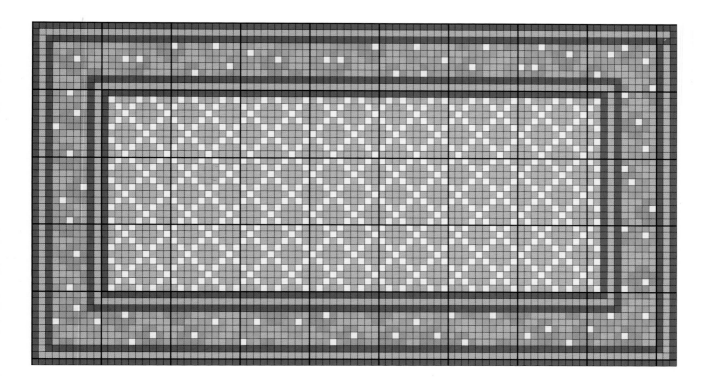

Variations

The long cushion design would also make a good stool top and vice versa, and an informal arrangement of different cushions would look good either on the bed or a sofa, or even on a window seat. The stool top could be extended to cover the top of a window seat – just make a long box out of wood or card!

Three different cushion designs are given in this chapter but it would be quite easy to come up with several others that tone in well. Try simply putting borders of colour around a plain centre (right).

The carpet could easily be enlarged by deepening the flowery border, which is easy to do as the design is random; you could also add further bands of plain colour. The look of the design is subtly changed by putting the pansies on the middle ground or 'inside' of the carpet (see page 62), or even by changing the cream border lines to dark blue (above). Similarly, flowers stitched in different colours would produce a completely different look to the same design (right). Experiment!

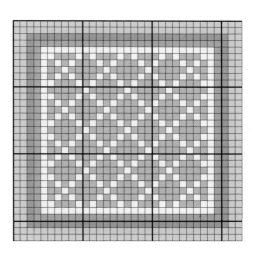

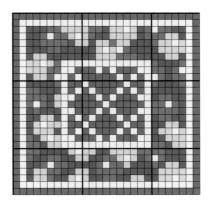

Chapter 5
**DINING
ROOM**

DINNER IS SERVED . . .

CHAPTER 5

DINNER IS SERVED...

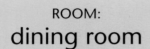

ROOM:
dining room

PROJECTS:
**large carpet
chair seat
three cushions**

DIFFICULTY RATING:
demanding

The delightful process of eating food is not only essential for our well-being, but is also often the central reason for many social events. However, we've come a long way from chewing on mammoth bones while squatting on the floor of a cave and exchanging companionable grunts with our neighbour (an early kind of indoor barbie?)

Early European manor houses used the large hall for almost every event in daily life, and presumably there would always be plenty of willing hands to put a few boards up on trestles at mealtimes. But when the rich landowners began to build their grand houses in the late 16th century they tended to include a small private dining chamber for the use of immediate family and friends – the rest of the household would still eat below, in the hall.

Rather than the make-shift trestle tables used downstairs, these private dining rooms would have a fixed table with large, bulbous legs joined by low stretchers. Since this was essentially a private room, other furniture was included for storing and displaying the family plate. This might be kept in an aumbry (which was a simple cupboard with doors), or in a court cupboard, which was not a cupboard at all but rather an ornate open shelf unit. Where the family was wealthy enough there might also be a carpet – but this was too good to be kept on the floor; it decorated the table. Altogether a rather confusing time!

By the end of the 17th century, furniture-makers began to produce furniture specifically to suit a separate 'dining' room. The gateleg table provided a large family table which could be folded away in a trice to provide extra space – providing, therefore, something in between the heavy fixed table and the DIY trestle tables of earlier times.

By the time 18th-century furniture designers had set to work on the dining room, its furnishings had become elegant, sophisticated and useful. Dining rooms were now often large, formal rooms, and tables were made with many extra leaves which could be inserted to suit the guest list, or dismantled to allow for a little dancing. In the Palladian style, which became increasingly popular, the kitchen was often a long way from the dining room; this gave birth to a rash of elegant serving tables and sideboards designed to keep food hot – or cold. Many were devised with separate ornamental pedestals which hid wine coolers, cutlery boxes, plate warmers, and even water for washing out glasses between courses.

In the 19th century, high society on both sides of the Atlantic elaborated on and developed the dinner party into a huge ritual meal. At the same time furniture became heavier and chunkier, and the colour schemes dark and rich. At this time the dining room was also often used as the gathering-place for family prayers.

Somehow between then and now the dining room has become just a second reception room which might be used for formal family events occasionally. These days many meals are taken in cosy kitchens, or on laps in front of the television. Maybe this is the result of smaller, more informal family units, or maybe it's a reaction to the busy lives we lead which emphasize our activities outside the home rather than within it.

For this dining room I have looked back to quieter, more elegant times, and married Chippendale chairs with an oriental design in blues and yellows. In western Europe the 18th century saw a tremendous interest in all things oriental, from tea drinking to garden design. The lattice or trellis influenced many designers working at this time, and the repeating swastika which makes up the border on this carpet represents happiness in Chinese culture. The yellow central ground is decorated with 'money' symbols in blue, so let's hope that stitching this design will bring you good fortune!

The 'family plate' was not a single platter to be shared by all family members, but a valuable collection of eating and drinking utensils made out of pewter, silver or gold – very much a status symbol.

You will need

For each project you will need size 26 needles, plus canvas and threads as listed below. Thread quantities are approximate, and you may well need less, but allow a little extra of the colours you wish to use to stitch up the finished cushions (e.g., if the cushion has a blue border then allow some extra of that blue to ladder-stitch your cushion to its backing).

Canvas sizes are approximate, so if you wish to use up odd pieces of canvas then check the finished sizes given – but do remember to leave a margin around your work for turnings.

PROJECT	22tpi canvas	THREAD LENGTHS PER COLOUR						Finished size
		Off white	Yellow	Tan	Garnet	Blue	White	
carpet	30 x 21cm	15m	25m	7m	1m	16m	2m	22 x 14.5cm
chair seat	10 x 10cm	2m	–	1m	–	1m	–	3.5 x 3.5cm*
cushion 1	10 x 10cm	1m	–	1m	0.5m	1m	–	3.1 x 3.1cm
cushion 2	10 x 10cm	–	1m	1m	–	1m	1m	3.1 x 3.1cm
cushion 3	10 x 10cm	–	1.5m	–	–	1.5m	–	3.1 x 3.1cm

• For imperial measurements please refer to the conversion chart on page 112 •
* As this is shaped, size is approximate

How to work the projects

Although the carpet is quite a large design, it's not as difficult as it may look at first sight. Much of the design is repetitive, so just take your time and refer to the pattern frequently. All the information you need for working the needlepoint is covered in the Basic Guide to Stitching (see page 10).

Cushion 1

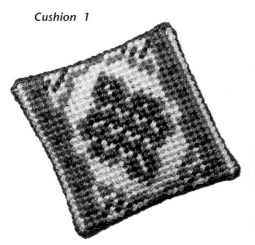

Charts for cushion 1

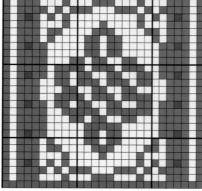

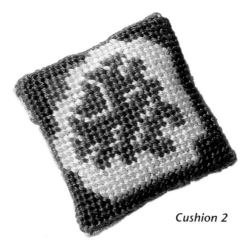

Cushion 2

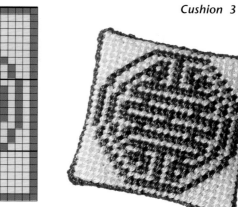

Cushion 3

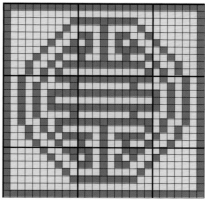

Charts for cushion 2

Charts for cushion 3

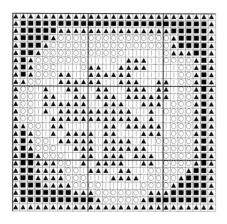

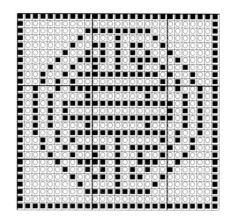

PROJECTS KEY		Anchor	DMC	Madeira
•	Off white	275	746	0101
○	Yellow	301	745	0112
▲	Tan	349	400	2306
▬	Garnet	44	814	0513
■	Blue	122	793	2702
∣	White	2	blanc	2402

Chair seat

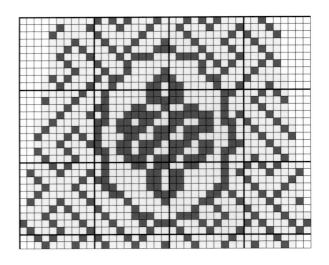

Charts for chair seat

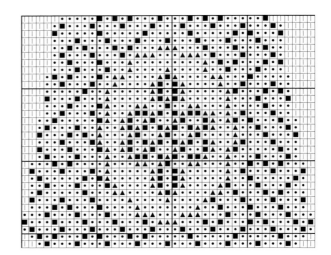

PROJECTS KEY			ANCHOR	DMC	MADEIRA
•	Off white		275	746	0101
○	Yellow		301	745	0112
▲	Tan		349	400	2306
▬	Garnet		44	814	0513
■	Blue		122	793	2702
ı	White		2	blanc	2402

Making up

For finishing all these projects see the Basic Guide to Finishing (page 16). You will need a piece of fusible interfacing to back the carpet, and fabric and stuffing for the cushions. You will also need either to make or to buy a chair to suit the chair seat.

Carpet

PROJECTS KEY	Anchor	DMC	Madeira
Off white	275	746	0101
Yellow	301	745	0112
Tan	349	400	2306

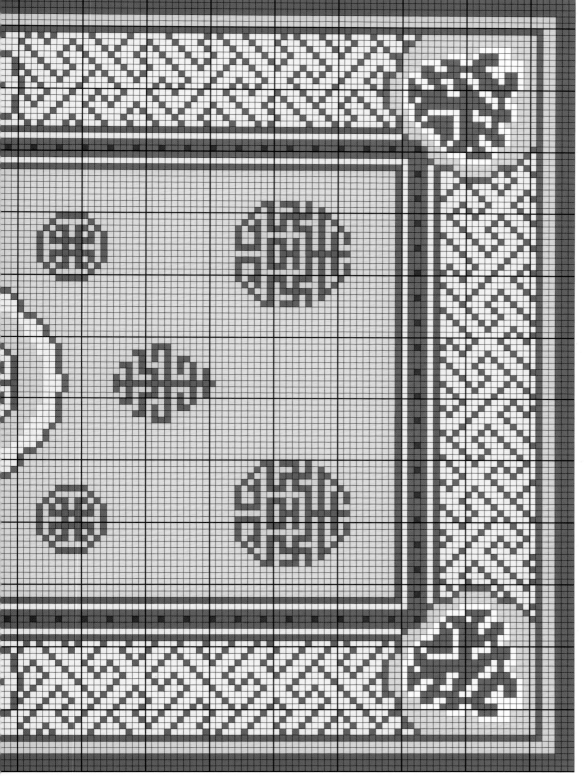

PROJECTS KEY	ANCHOR	DMC	MADEIRA
Garnet	44	814	0513
Blue	122	793	2702
White	2	blanc	2402

PROJECTS KEY		ANCHOR	DMC	MADEIRA
•	Off white	275	746	0101
○	Yellow	301	745	0112
◄	Tan	349	400	2306

PROJECTS KEY	Anchor	DMC	Madeira
▮ Garnet	44	814	0513
■ Blue	122	793	2702
— White	2	blanc	2402

Variations

You can, of course, vary any of the colours to suit your own decor, but since it's an oriental design it looks most fitting in oriental colours – blue, green, yellow, brown, rust, cream etc. The yellow ground is very dominant, so you could tone it down to a cream and perhaps replace the tan with a softer brown.

The carpet can easily be reduced in size by omitting the trellis-work border but retaining the outer blue band, and perhaps adding an extra row of blue for balance (right). This also makes it very easy to work!

Another cushion idea is shown on the left; this can also be used to make an alternative chair seat. Place the central motif in the middle of your chair seat, continuing with the brown background until the chair seat is covered.

Similarly, the blue trellis chair seat can be extended to make a sofa seat. Below the motif is shown sideways and repeated, the background being filled in with trellis work. I'm sure that you'll be able to come up with many more ideas by pulling out various parts of the carpet design or playing with the colours.

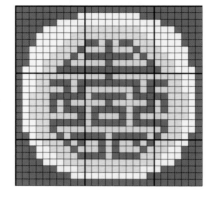

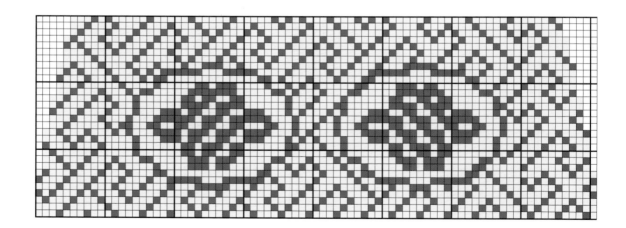

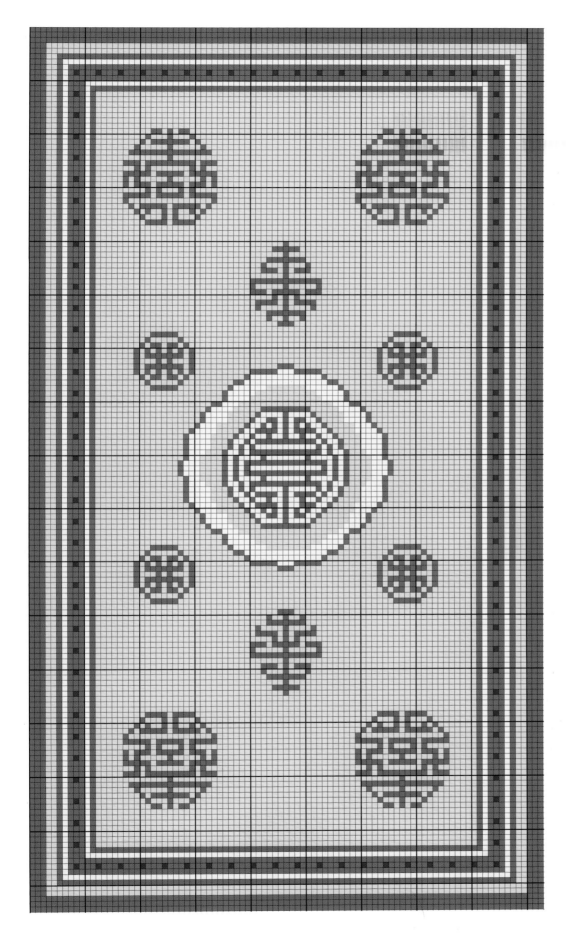

Chapter 6
LIBRARY

HERE BE DRAGONS . . .

CHAPTER 6

HERE BE DRAGONS...

ROOM:

library

PROJECTS:

carpet
chair seat
two cushions
picture

DIFFICULTY RATING:

demanding

If you're lucky enough to have a large dolls' house, then you're probably wondering what to do with all those extra rooms. Of course, you could just have more bedrooms – but why not have something a little different? A library is so easy to create. Obviously you'll need lots of books and somewhere to store them, but this doesn't mean that you need to have expensive bookcases. It's not difficult to make simple shelving and perhaps add wooden mouldings at the edges to suggest a grander bookcase. Add some comfy chairs, side tables – and maybe a desk if you have space. Accessories could include lots of pictures, maps and table lamps to give an intimate glow. The inclusion of a globe and a telescope would suggest that the occupant of the house is a well-travelled and educated fellow.

Before the development of printing in the mid 15th century books were very rare indeed, and consequently far too valuable to be left lying about the home. Even after the development of printing it was nearly a hundred years before book-owning became more widespread, and books were still considered a luxury item. A wealthy gentleman would not possess more than fifty or sixty books at most.

In the late 16th and early 17th centuries a gentleman would keep any books he owned in his 'closet.' This was not a walk-in cupboard, but a small room off his bedchamber which he used for his personal possessions such as papers, cash, weapons, maps etc. A book was still a personal treasure rather than a part of the general household furnishings.

If we move on another century, we find that the gradual expansion of education meant that books were in greater demand; also, quicker and cheaper printing methods led to more widespread book ownership. Books were still valuable possessions, though, and so needed special furniture to store and protect them. The master furniture designers rose to the occasion and produced a variety of bookcases, breakfronts, bureaux and cabinets to fill this gap in the market. Naturally these bookcases were far too grand for a gentleman's closet, so a new room had to be found; the library was born.

Initially the library was used just as a study, but in large 18th-century houses it often became a sort of informal family sitting room. Books were to be found even in the houses of the less well-educated gentry, though they were still valuable enough to be considered as status symbols, and were often stamped with a family crest.

In England in the 19th century the Victorians included the library into their establishments with few if any changes, except that it was usually now located on the ground floor. The Arts and Crafts Movement in the 1860s looked back to the age of chivalry, courtly love and all things mediaeval, so these dragons fit well into a Victorian library, and the vibrant colours lend life to the typical dark furnishings of the time.

Today many of us have a 'home office' or study with the omnipresent computer, and Americans have their much-loved 'den', but I think that it must have been rather nice to have a library – a quiet room full of lovely books, and a comfortable armchair in a sunlit corner.

Bess of Hardwick, one of the great English Elizabethans, married at the age of 12 and worked her way through four husbands who each endowed her with their wealth. This she used to build the wonderful Hardwick Hall in Derbyshire – but nevertheless she only possessed 6 books!

My dragon is a feisty chap clad in splendid royal red and sporting impressive blue wings. The square cushion is slightly larger than other cushions in this book, to accommodate the dragon's tail; you can of course make the outer border blue if you prefer. The long cushion uses a

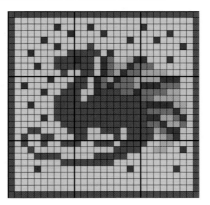

blue border plus a little fancy pattern as a contrast. The carpet sets a pair of dragons on a speckled gold ground with a dramatic wide border, and the little dragon picture offers a change of mood.

DRAGON TRIVIA
Dragon was the celtic word for chief: thus King Arthur, of round table fame, was called Arthur Pendragon. In Mediaeval times the serpent or dragon was the symbol of sin, therefore all knights were honour-bound to seek out and destroy the beasts, but Henry VII of England took the dragon as his standard; as 'royal' dragons they became respectable again.

You will need

For each project you will need size 26 needles, plus canvas and threads as listed below. Thread quantities are approximate, and you may well need less, but allow an extra piece of thread in the appropriate colour if you wish to use it to stitch up the finished cushions.

Canvas sizes are approximate, so if you wish to use up odd pieces of canvas then check the finished sizes given – but do remember to leave a margin around your work for turnings.

PROJECT	22tpi canvas	THREAD LENGTHS PER COLOUR								Finished size
		Off white	Gold	Pale blue	Mid blue	Dark blue	Green	Dark green	Red	Dark red	
carpet	17 x 13cm	–	5.5m	1m	1m	5.5m	–	–	4m	2m	10.8 x 6.9cm
long cushion	10 x 10cm	–	2m	1m	1m	2m	–	–	1m	–	4.5 x 3.1cm
sq. cushion	10 x 10cm	–	2m	1m	1m	1m	–	–	1.5m	–	3.2 x 3.2cm
chair seat	10 x 10cm	–	2.5m	1m	1m	1m	–	–	1m	–	3.5 x 3.5cm*
picture	10 x 10cm	1m	1m	1m	1m	1m	1.5m	1m	1m	–	4.9 x 2.8cm

• For imperial measurements please refer to the conversion chart on page 112•
* As this is shaped, size is approximate

How to work the projects

To work all the projects, follow the stitching instructions given in the Basic Guide to Stitching (see page 10). The blue flecks on the gold background are random, so don't worry if you go astray. The border on the carpet needs careful attention, and so does the dragon's wing, so save these tasks for quiet moments when you can concentrate well!

PROJECTS KEY		Anchor	DMC	Madeira
+	Off white	275	746	0101
•	Gold	311	725	2513
=	Pale blue	117	341	0901
O	Mid blue	122	793	2702
▲	Dark blue	123	791	0914
◢	Green	261	368	1401
●	Dark green	210	562	1206
■	Red	44	815	0513
＼	Dark red	45	814	0601

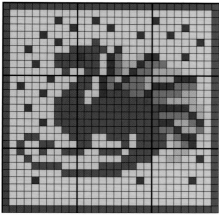

*Square
cushion*

Charts for square cushion

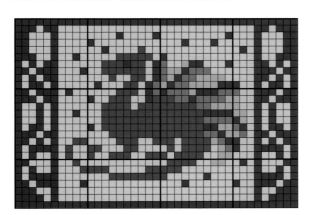

Long cushion

Charts for long cushion

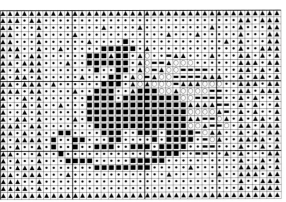

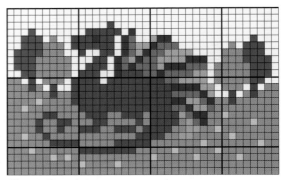

Charts for picture

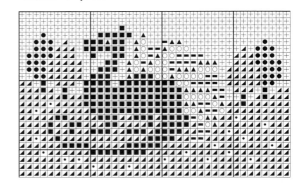

PROJECTS KEY		ANCHOR	DMC	MADEIRA
+	Off white	275	746	0101
•	Gold	311	725	2513
−	Pale blue	117	341	0901
O	Mid blue	122	793	2702
▲	Dark blue	123	791	0914
◢	Green	261	368	1401
●	Dark green	210	562	1206
■	Red	44	815	0513
\	Dark red	45	814	0601

Chair seat

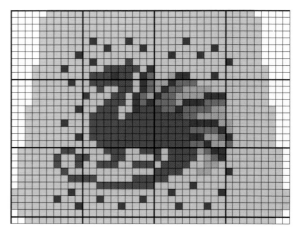

Charts for chair seat

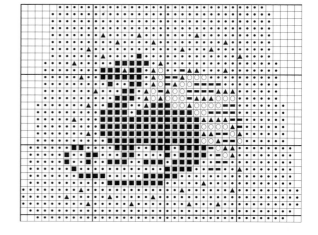

Picture

Making up

For finishing all these projects see the Basic Guide to Finishing (page 16). You will need a small piece of fusible interfacing to back the carpet, and fabric and stuffing for the cushions.

Colour chart for carpet

Symbols chart for carpet

Carpet

PROJECTS KEY		ANCHOR	DMC	MADEIRA
+	Off white	275	746	0101
•	Gold	311	725	2513
▬	Pale blue	117	341	0901
O	Mid blue	122	793	2702
▲	Dark blue	123	791	0914
◢	Green	261	368	1401
●	Dark green	210	562	1206
■	Red	44	815	0513
＼	Dark red	45	814	0601

Variations

The long cushion and the picture would also make excellent footstools – just make a little frame for them, or fold the stitching around a small block of wood and use wooden beads for feet.

This series of designs uses three main colours – red, blue and gold – which makes it easy to vary the colour scheme. To maintain the drama keep to rich, contrasting jewel colours; you could experiment with purple, green or jade (right). The wing has three graduated shades of one colour – in this case blue. If you wanted the dragon to have wings of another colour, you'd obviously need to pick three toning shades; I've done this, using reds, for the little green dragon shown below right. You'll see that I've also experimented by giving some shading to his body with darker greens – but this of course makes him more complex to stitch!

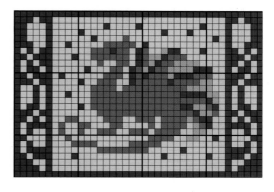

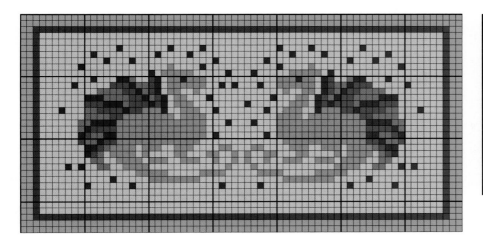

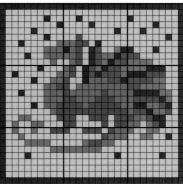

A BOUQUET OF ROSES . . .

CHAPTER 7

A BOUQUET OF ROSES...

ROOM:
drawing room

PROJECTS:
large carpet
sofa and chair seats
three cushions

DIFFICULTY RATING:
demanding

What is a drawing room? The name has its origins in the term with-drawing room, the room to which the family retired away from the hurly-burly of the main hall. As a child I used to think that a drawing room must be something like the Art Room at school, and thought how lucky grand people were to have a room set aside just for drawing. Of course we didn't have a drawing room in our house – or an art room come to that; we had a 'sitting room' which was where we all gathered at the end of the day to be comfortable. Such a room may now also be called a living room or a lounge.

We've probably all seen pictures or old photos of turn-of-the-century drawing rooms, those large grandiose rooms cluttered with furniture. In England the Victorians were good at inventing furniture, and their drawing rooms would contain a variety of sofas and armchairs, side chairs, card-tables, tea-tables, footstools, display cabinets and whatnots, not to mention a piano (suitably draped, of course, to conceal its shapely and seductive legs). Every surface would carry its burden of ornaments and a veritable jungle of pot plants.

Perhaps I'm being very rude about Victorian decor – and maybe this is your favourite period? After all, most miniaturists have a favourite decorative era. But if I could go back in time to sit in a drawing room, then I would bid my time machine take me back to the end of the 18th century.

Unashamedly the grandest room in the house, the drawing room of this era was situated on the first floor and approached up a sweep of stairs; beside the staircase might hang the portraits of the host's ancestors, so that guests had time to be suitably impressed before even making their bows and curtseys. (I can't help thinking that they'd be even more disadvantaged by being out of breath after climbing those long staircases.) The drawing room was used for entertaining, parties, dancing, musical soirées etc, and was the room for making an impression and showing off your wealth. Here would be displayed the best of your paintings and ornamental porcelain in a room which would be well-lit for the purpose. The decor would be both tasteful and sumptuous, with ornate ceilings, gorgeous carpets, gilded mirrors, sparkling chandeliers and elegant furniture.

So for my drawing room projects I've turned to my favourite pink colour-scheme, and looked back to the glorious floral designs of the 18th century. These could be found on the porcelain from famous English factories such as Royal Worcester, which by the late 1760s was producing designs with typical blue grounds, shaped panels and floral decorations. Other rich colours such as turquoise, claret, yellow and green were also used, and designs were further embellished with gilding. The vogue for such designs spread across Europe and was also reflected in the carpets produced in France at this time, most notably at Aubusson.

Situated in a traditional weaving area of central France, the town of Aubusson was near to Limoges, renowned for its porcelain. Aubusson was granted Royal Manufactory status in 1665, and towards the end of the 18th century its output had increased considerably to meet the tremendous demand for tapestry wall-hangings and furniture coverings. Floral-patterned carpets, echoing the popular designs already seen on porcelain, were being produced, and this is the style which I have tried to create with the designs in this chapter.

The overblown flowers suggest opulence, and the pinks and creams are enhanced by the delicate gold scrolls, which imitate the gilding found on ceiling and wall decorations. The flowers do need careful attention while you're stitching them, but there are straight bands of colour around the edges and large areas of cream on the centre ground to compensate – and once you see the carpet growing you'll be eager to finish it!

In past times the drawing room was thought of as a 'feminine' room, just as the dining room was a 'masculine' room.

You will need

For each project you will need size 26 needles, plus canvas and threads as listed below. Thread quantities are approximate, and you may well need less, but allow an extra piece of thread in the appropriate colour if you wish to use it to stitch up the finished cushions.

Canvas sizes are approximate, so if you wish to use up odd pieces of canvas then check the finished sizes given – but do remember to leave a margin around your work for turnings.

PROJECT	22tpi canvas	THREAD LENGTHS PER COLOUR							Finished size
		Off white	Gold	Old gold	Pale pink	Pink	Maroon	Khaki green	
carpet	30 x 25cm	24.5m	10.5m	8.5m	2.5m	10.5m	12m	6m	20 x 16.7cm
cushion 1	10 x 10cm	1.5m	1m	1m	1m	1m	1m	1m	3.1 x 3.1cm
cushion 2	10 x 10cm	1.5m	–	–	1m	1m	1m	1m	3.1 x 3.1cm
cushion 3	10 x 10cm	1m	1m	1m	1m	1m	1m	1m	3.1 x 3.1cm
chair seat	10 x 10cm	1m	1m	1m	1m	1.5m	1m	1m	4 x 3.5cm*
sofa seat	15 x 9cm	1.5m	1.5m	1.5m	1m	3m	1m	1m	9.2 x 3.7cm*

• For imperial measurements please refer to the conversion chart on page 112 •
* As these are shaped, sizes are approximate

How to work the projects

For all the projects, follow the Basic Guide to Stitching (see page 10). You might prefer to start with a cushion before tackling the carpet. As the carpet is large and has a detailed design, do take your bearings regularly. By this I mean, keep checking that each part of the design is in the right place; you can do this by counting stitches back to a point of reference you know is correct, such as the edge of the carpet or a border.

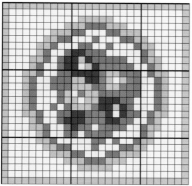

Charts for cushion 1

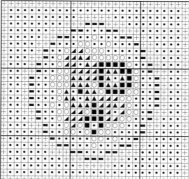

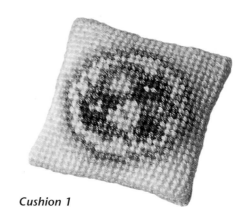

Cushion 1

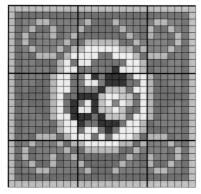

Charts for cushion 2

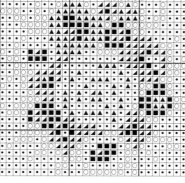

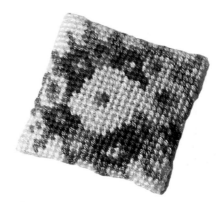

Cushion 2

Charts for cushion 3

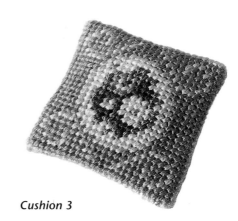

Cushion 3

PROJECTS KEY			ANCHOR	DMC	MADEIRA
	•	Off white	275	746	0101
	+	Gold	311	725	2513
	−	Old gold	901	680	2210
	▲	Pale pink	1010	3746	2308
	■	Pink	895	223	0812
	◣	Maroon	897	221	2606
	○	Khaki green	843	3012	1606

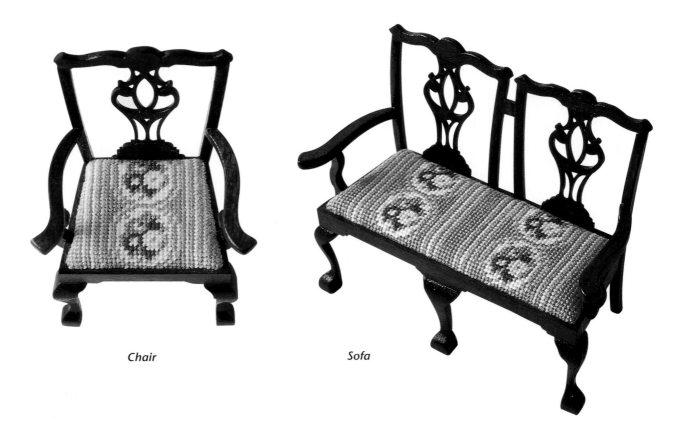

Chair

Sofa

Charts for chair seat

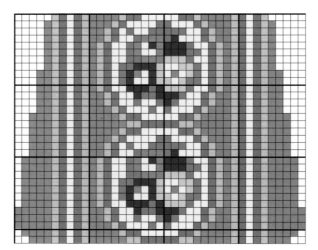

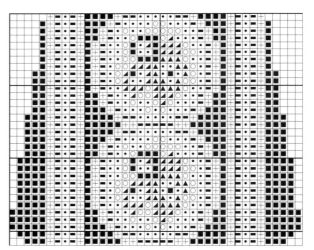

PROJECTS KEY			ANCHOR	DMC	MADEIRA
■	•	Off white	275	746	0101
■	+	Gold	311	725	2513
■	▬	Old gold	901	680	2210
■	▲	Pale pink	1010	3746	2308
■	■	Pink	895	223	0812
■	◀	Maroon	897	221	2606
■	○	Khaki green	843	3012	1606

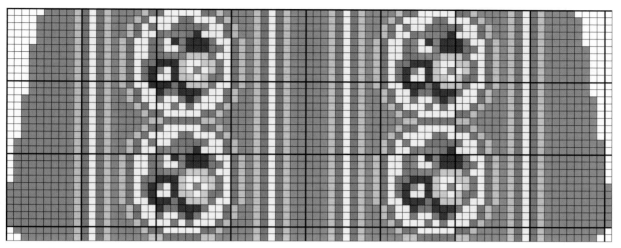

Charts for sofa seat

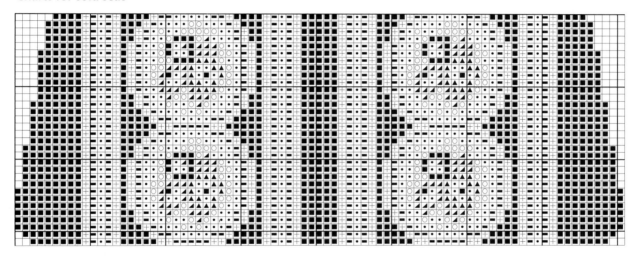

Making up

For finishing all the projects see the Basic Guide to
Finishing (page 16). You will need fusible interfacing to
back the carpet, and fabric and stuffing for the cushions.
The sofa (love seat) and chairs in the photographs have
been assembled from kits and finished by my useful
husband.

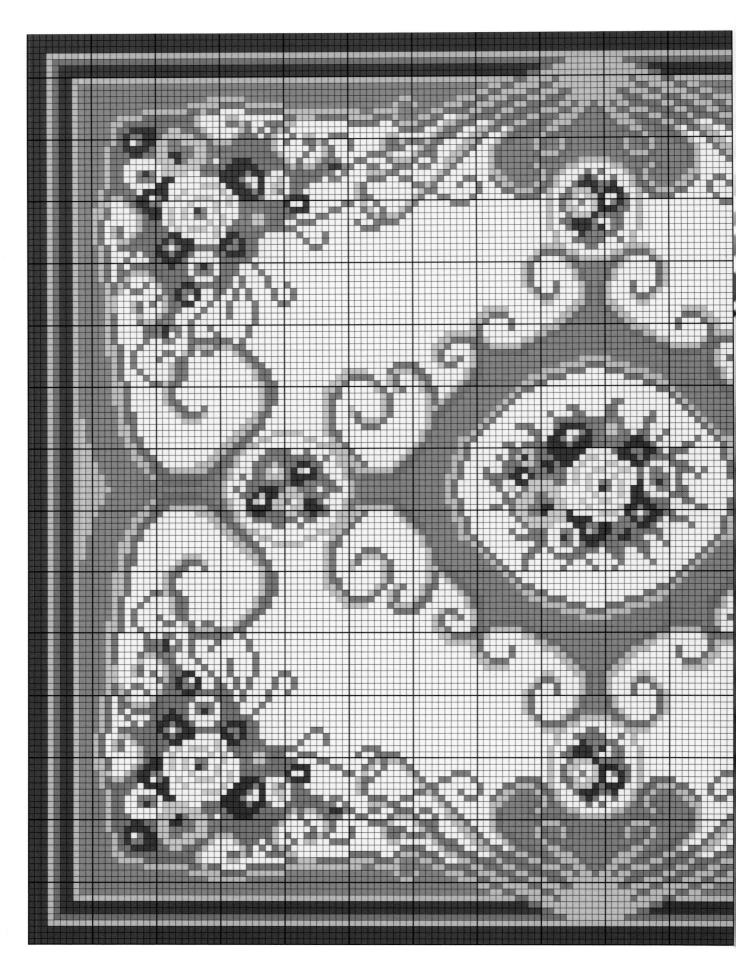

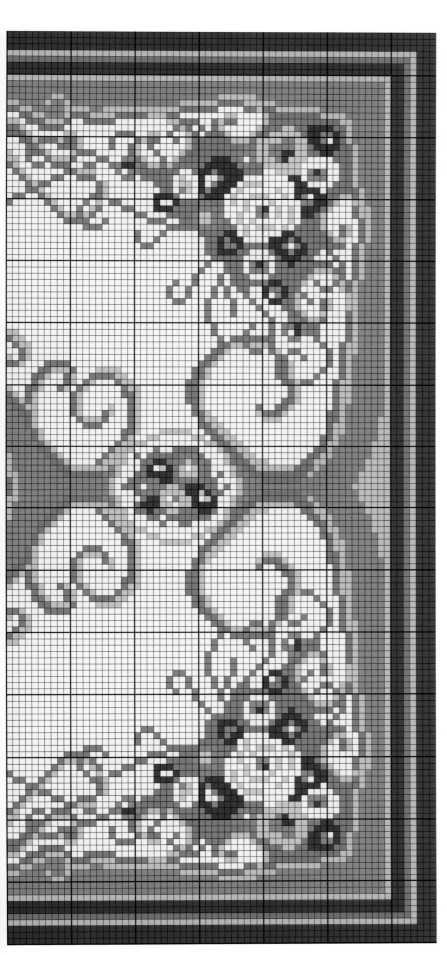

PROJECTS KEY	ANCHOR	DMC	MADEIRA
Off white	275	746	0101
Gold	311	725	2513
Old gold	901	680	2210
Pale pink	1010	3746	2308
Pink	895	223	0812
Maroon	897	221	2606
Khaki green	843	3012	1606

**Colour chart
for carpet**

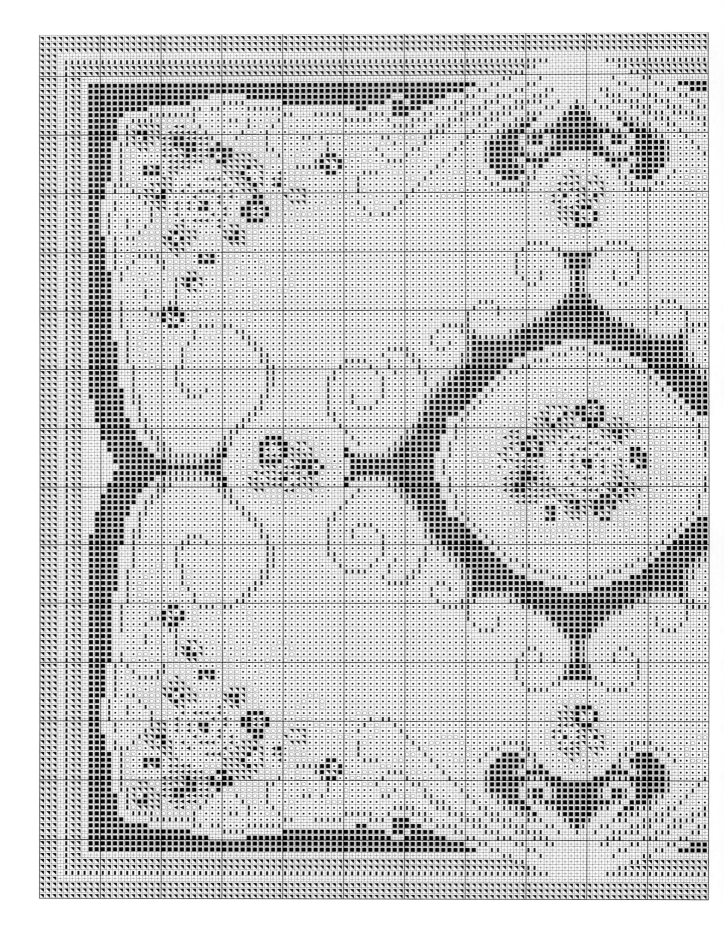

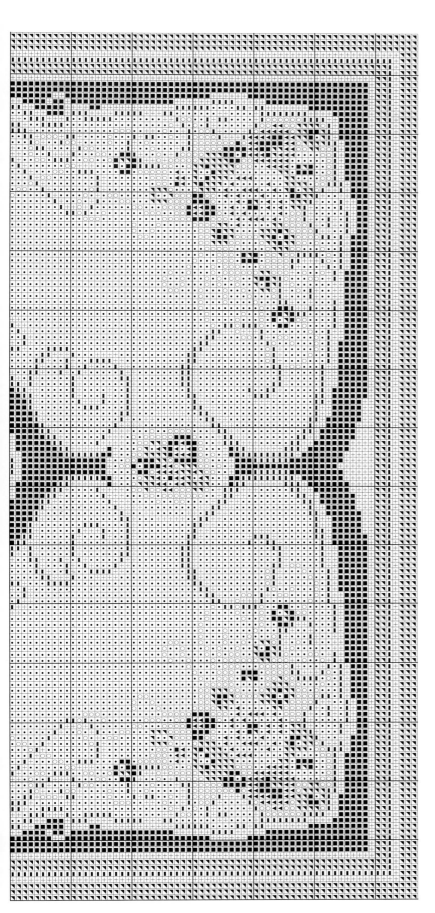

PROJECTS KEY	ANCHOR	DMC	MADEIRA
• Off white	275	746	0101
+ Gold	311	725	2513
▌ Old gold	901	680	2210
◀ Pale pink	1010	3746	2308
■ Pink	895	223	0812
◥ Maroon	897	221	2606
○ Khaki green	843	3012	1606

**Symbols chart
for carpet**

> *This carpet does look difficult to stitch, and I wouldn't recommend it to the novice. But just as every journey begins with one step, so every carpet begins with one stitch – and then another; and then, in this case, a little over 26,000 stitches!*

Carpet

Variations

If you've arrived at this point by reading through the rest of the book, you'll probably already have some good notions on how to customize these designs to suit your own purposes. However, for those of you who read magazines and reference books backwards (as I do!) I will make a few suggestions.

There are three square cushions shown, any of which could be enlarged to make long cushions, chair seats, footstools or a piano-stool top. The central bouquet of the carpet would also make a delightful fire screen.

If you are daunted by the size of the carpet – why not try a smaller version? Eliminate the big bunches of flowers in the corners and the side scrolls, and smooth out the edges (right). Draw out a corner on graph paper before starting to stitch.

You can make dramatic changes to this design by simply changing the pinks to shades of a different colour. Remember that there are three pinks – pale, medium and dark – so you will need to replace these with three similar tones of your chosen colour. You could shade from lilac through to purple, or work in shades of turquoise, green or red. I think that blue also works very well; I've used it for the variation shown on pages 106–109. Keep the colours bold and dramatic, though; I think that, having done all that hard work, you deserve to end up with a carpet that knocks their socks off!

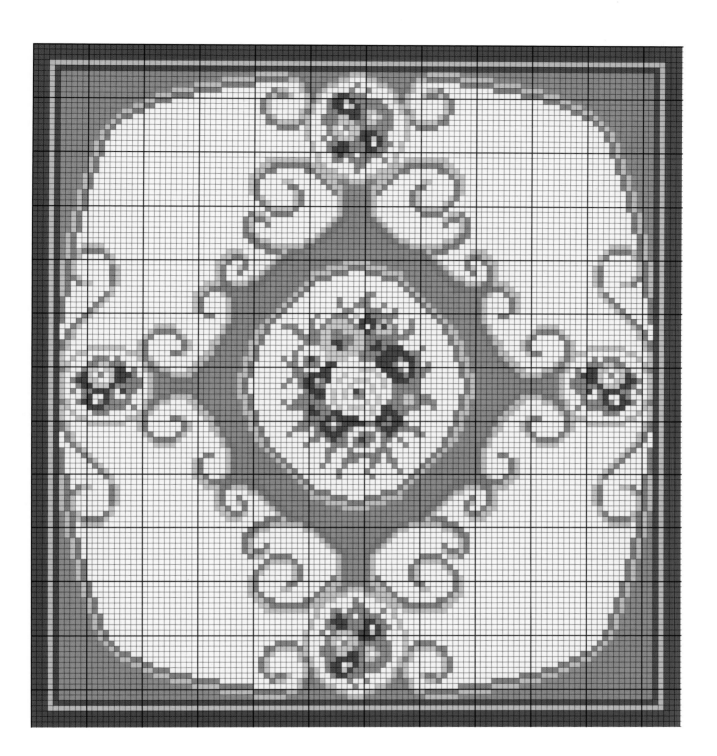

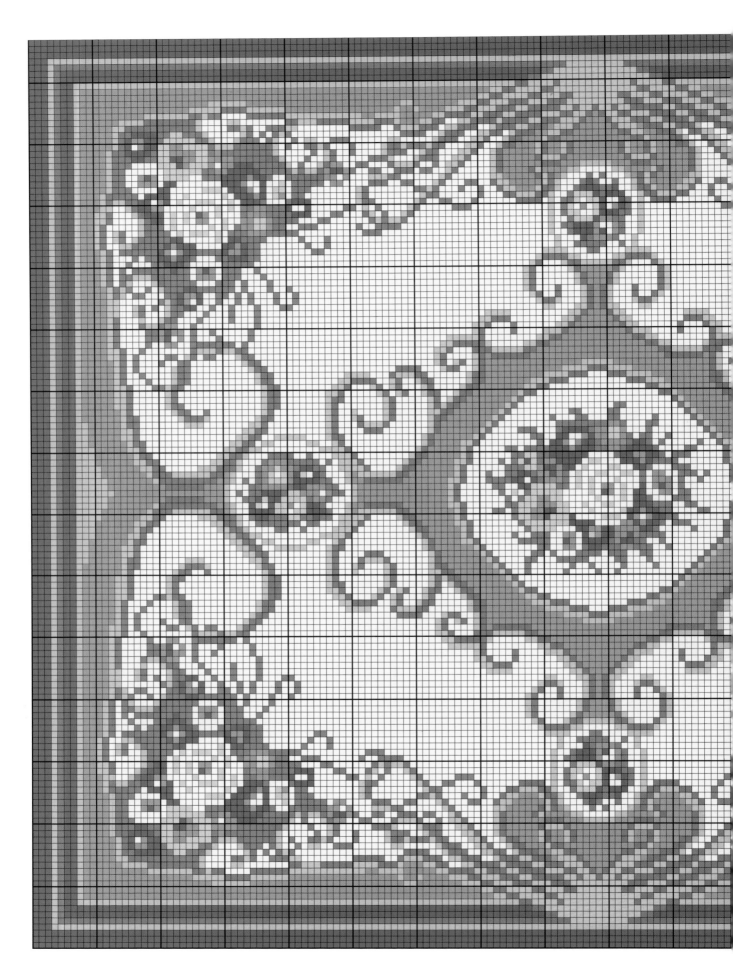

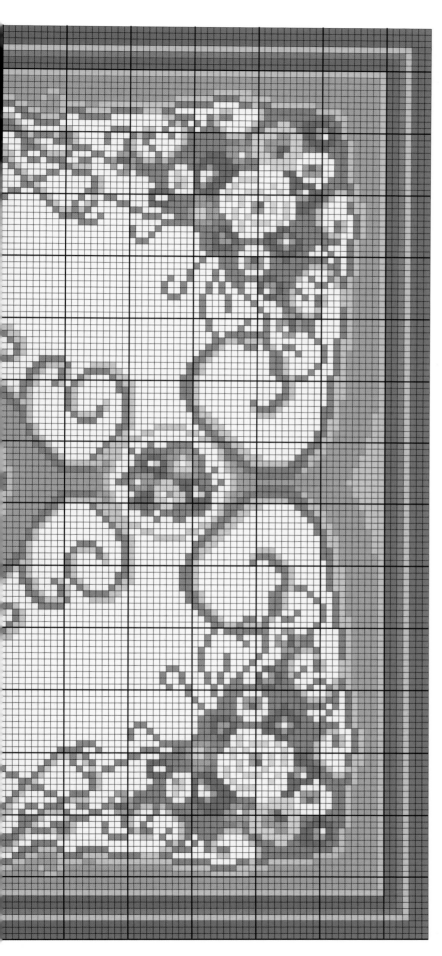

VARIATION KEY	ANCHOR	DMC	MADEIRA
Off white	275	746	0101
Gold	311	725	2513
Old gold	901	680	2210
Pale blue	120	794	0909
Blue	121	809	0906
Dark blue	123	791	0914
Khaki green	843	3012	1606

**Colour chart
for blue carpet**

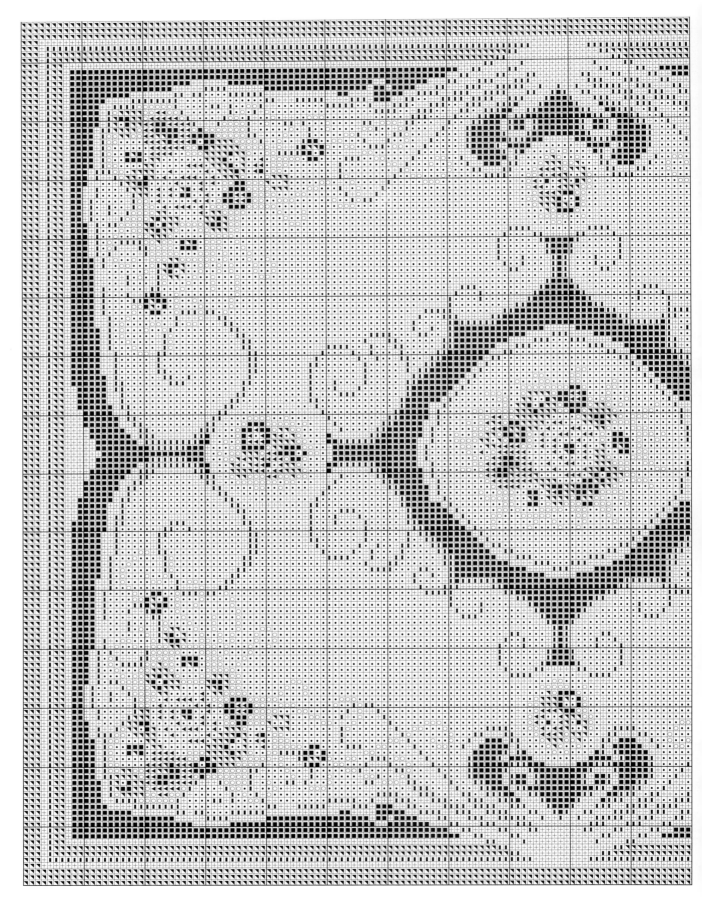

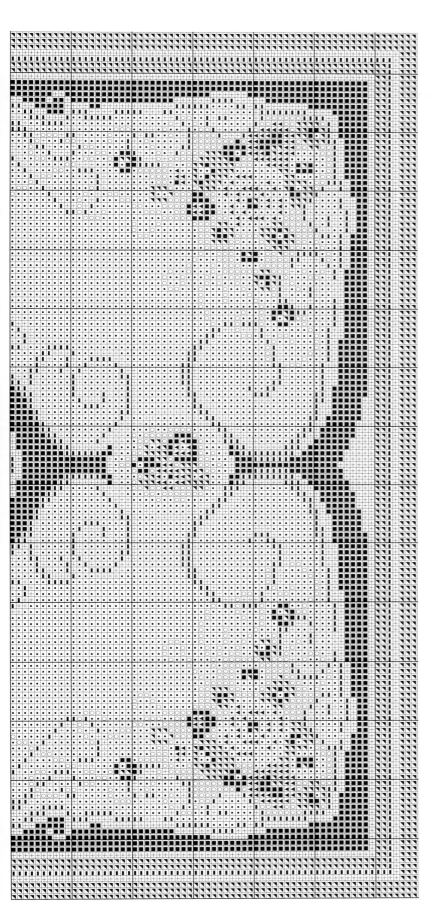

VARIATION KEY	Anchor	DMC	Madeira
• Off white	275	746	0101
+ Gold	311	725	2513
▌ Old gold	901	680	2210
◀ Pale blue	120	794	0909
■ Blue	121	809	0906
◥ Dark blue	123	791	0914
○ Khaki green	843	3012	1606

**Symbols chart
for blue carpet**

GENERAL INFORMATION & ACKNOWLEDGEMENTS

Canvas, thread, needles and scissors

These are widely available from needlework shops. Remember to look for 22 tpi cotton canvas, size 26 tapestry needles and 'embroidery' scissors. Anchor stranded cotton threads have been used to make all the projects in the book, but if these are not available or if you prefer to use alternatives then you will find the closest available matches listed on the keys for each project – remember that the closest colour from another manufacturer may produce slight colour variations in your finished work.

Tools

Magnifying glasses and needlework frames can be bought from good specialist needlework shops, and opticians usually offer magnifying glasses which can be hung around your neck. Hobby shops often sell magnifying lights which can be attached to your work table, and are generally a good source of other helpful gadgets.

Stationery

Graph paper and children's arithmetic books are useful for sketching out a design, and a pack of coloured pencils is essential to help you get the right colour balance: try any stationery shop for these items.

Computer

Designing on graph paper is fine for most purposes, but if you're computer-friendly then you might like to try designing on your computer. There are a number of software packages available to help you do this, but remember that they are designed for life-size projects, so make sure that the program allows you to get really close up to the design.

Ursa Software produce a number of design products and they have proved invariably helpful with all my queries over the years. They can be contacted at:
Ursa Software, 17 Camborne Grove, Gateshead, Tyne & Wear NE8 4EX (UK).

Furniture and accessories

Most of the furniture and accessories used in this book have been supplied by Small Comfort of Fleetwood, Lancashire (UK). The Chippendale chairs and sofa used have been put together from House of Miniature kits; these are widely available from good miniature shops, as are the stools, toybox and most of the accessories. A special thankyou to my husband, Harry, who lovingly assembled the chair and sofa kits. He was also cajoled into making a few specific pieces of furniture for the book, such as the hall stand and bedroom furniture.

Needlework kits

All needlework projects shown in this book are also available as kits from the address listed below under 'help'. The catalogue (£2.50 for the UK, £3.50 for the rest of the world) includes stitching kits, canvas, needles, furniture kits etc. (US residents please contact Miniature Needleworks Inc, PO Box 1444, Montauk, NY 11954).

Help

For help or advice please write to me including a stamped addressed envelope: Felicity Price, 21 West Drive, Cleveleys, Lancashire FY5 2BJ.

Conversion chart

inches to millimetres

inches	mm	inches	mm	inches	mm
⅛	3	9	229	30	762
¼	6	10	254	31	787
⅜	10	11	279	32	813
½	13	12	305	33	838
⅝	16	13	330	34	864
¾	19	14	356	35	889
⅞	22	15	381	36	914
1	25	16	406	37	940
1¼	32	17	432	38	965
1½	38	18	457	39	991
1¾	44	19	483	40	1016
2	51	20	508	41	1041
2½	64	21	533	42	1067
3	76	22	559	43	1092
3½	89	23	584	44	1118
4	102	24	610	45	1143
4½	114	25	635	46	1168
5	127	26	660	47	1194
6	152	27	686	48	1219
7	178	28	711	49	1245
8	203	29	737	50	1270

About the author

Felicity Price has been interested in craftwork all her adult life. She was first introduced to the world of miniatures when her husband made a Tudor dolls' house as a woodworking exercise. In the early 80s the hobby was in its infancy and it was difficult to interest people in needlework for dolls' houses, so she turned her attention to home and family; but she was already hooked on miniatures, and continued to research and experiment with designs.

As soon as family pressures permitted Felicity developed the Small Comfort range of needlepoint kits. Realising that there was a dearth of miniatures in her region, she then started a retail miniatures business; her work includes attending fairs and she has also completed a number of private commissions.

Three years ago she began writing on miniature needlepoint for specialist magazines, with articles appearing regularly in dolls' house periodicals. She lives in Fleetwood in Lancashire, with her husband, son and three cats.

INDEX

Page numbers marked *t* refer to text in boxes.

Woodturning Tools & Equipment Test Reports   GMC Publications
Woodturning Wizardry   David Springett

WOODWORKING

Advanced Scrollsaw Projects   GMC Publications
Beginning Picture Marquetry   Lawrence Threadgold
Bird Boxes and Feeders for the Garden   Dave Mackenzie
Complete Woodfinishing   Ian Hosker
David Charlesworth's Furniture-Making Techniques   David Charlesworth
David Charlesworth's Furniture-Making Techniques – Volume 2   David Charlesworth
The Encyclopedia of Joint Making   Terrie Noll
Furniture-Making Projects for the Wood Craftsman   GMC Publications
Furniture-Making Techniques for the Wood Craftsman   GMC Publications
Furniture Projects   Rod Wales
Furniture Restoration (Practical Crafts)   Kevin Jan Bonner
Furniture Restoration: A Professional at Work   John Lloyd
Furniture Restoration and Repair for Beginners   Kevin Jan Bonner
Furniture Restoration Workshop   Kevin Jan Bonner
Green Woodwork   Mike Abbott
The History of Furniture   Michael Huntley
Intarsia: 30 Patterns for the Scrollsaw   John Everett
Kevin Ley's Furniture Projects   Kevin Ley
Making & Modifying Woodworking Tools   Jim Kingshott
Making Chairs and Tables   GMC Publications
Making Chairs and Tables – Volume 2   GMC Publications
Making Classic English Furniture   Paul Richardson
Making Heirloom Boxes   Peter Lloyd
Making Little Boxes from Wood   John Bennett
Making Screw Threads in Wood   Fred Holder
Making Shaker Furniture   Barry Jackson
Making Woodwork Aids and Devices   Robert Wearing
Mastering the Router   Ron Fox
Minidrill: Fifteen Projects   John Everett
Pine Furniture Projects for the Home   Dave Mackenzie
Practical Scrollsaw Patterns   John Everett
Router Magic: Jigs, Fixtures and Tricks to
  Unleash your Router's Full Potential   Bill Hylton
Router Tips & Techniques   GMC Publications
Routing: A Workshop Handbook   Anthony Bailey
Routing for Beginners   Anthony Bailey
The Scrollsaw: Twenty Projects   John Everett
Sharpening: The Complete Guide   Jim Kingshott
Sharpening Pocket Reference Book   Jim Kingshott
Simple Scrollsaw Projects   GMC Publications
Space-Saving Furniture Projects   Dave Mackenzie
Stickmaking: A Complete Course   Andrew Jones & Clive George
Stickmaking Handbook   Andrew Jones & Clive George
Storage Projects for the Router   GMC Publications
Test Reports: *The Router* and *Furniture & Cabinetmaking*   GMC Publications
Veneering: A Complete Course   Ian Hosker
Veneering Handbook   Ian Hosker
Woodfinishing Handbook (Practical Crafts)   Ian Hosker
Woodworking with the Router: Professional
  Router Techniques any Woodworker can Use   Bill Hylton & Fred Matlack
The Workshop   Jim Kingshott

UPHOLSTERY

The Upholsterer's Pocket Reference Book   David James
Upholstery: A Complete Course (Revised Edition)   David James
Upholstery Restoration   David James
Upholstery Techniques & Projects   David James
Upholstery Tips and Hints   David James

TOYMAKING

Restoring Rocking Horses   Clive Green & Anthony Dew
Scrollsaw Toy Projects   Ivor Carlyle
Scrollsaw Toys for All Ages   Ivor Carlyle

DOLLS' HOUSES AND MINIATURES

CRAFTS

GARDENING

PHOTOGRAPHY

MAGAZINES

WOODTURNING ◆ WOODCARVING ◆ FURNITURE & CABINETMAKING ◆ THE ROUTER
WOODWORKING ◆ THE DOLLS' HOUSE MAGAZINE ◆ WATER GARDENING
OUTDOOR PHOTOGRAPHY ◆ BLACK & WHITE PHOTOGRAPHY ◆ BUSINESSMATTERS

The above represents a full list of all titles currently published or scheduled to be published. All are available direct from the Publishers or through bookshops, newsagents and specialist retailers.

To place an order, or to obtain a complete catalogue, contact:

GMC Publications,
Castle Place, 166 High Street, Lewes East Sussex BN7 1XU, United Kingdom
Tel: 01273 488005 Fax: 01273 478606 E-mail: pubs@thegmcgroup.com

Orders by credit card are accepted